646.7
Fuentes, Daisy.
Unforgettable you : master the
elements of style, spirituality,
2010.

Unforgettable You

Unforgettable You

You

Master the Elements of Style, Spirituality, and True Beauty

DAISY FUENTES

ATRIA BOOKS
NEW YORK LONDON TORONTO SYDNEY

ATRIA BOOKS
A Division of Simon & Schuster, Inc.
1230 Avenue of the Americas
New York, NY 10020

Copyright © 2010 by Daisy Fuentes

First Atria Books hardcover edition May 2010

ATRIA BOOKS and colophon are trademarks of Simon & Schuster, Inc.

For information about special discounts for bulk purchases, please contact Simon & Schuster Special Sales at 1-866-506-1949 or business@simonandschuster.com.

The Simon & Schuster Speakers Bureau can bring authors to your live event. For more information or to book an event contact the Simon & Schuster Speakers Bureau at 1-866-248-3049 or visit our website at www.simonspeakers.com.

Designed by Davina Mock-Maniscalco

Manufactured in the United States of America

10 9 8 7 6 5 4 3 2 1

Library of Congress Cataloging-in-Publication Data

Fuentes, Daisy.
  Unforgettable you: master the elements of style, spirituality, and true beauty/ Daisy Fuentes.
    p. cm.
  1. Beauty, Personal. 2. Beauty, Personal—Social aspects—United States. 3. Beauty, Personal—Technique. I. Title.
HQ1219.F84 2010
646.7—dc22   2009032341

ISBN 978-1-4165-6301-3
ISBN 978-1-4165-6325-9 (ebook)

Dedicated to Mary and Amado
aka Mami and Papi

Unforgettable, that's what you are,
Unforgettable though near or far
—Irving Gordon

Contents
· · · · · · · · · ·

CONTENTS

Preface

"I did but see her passing by . . .
And yet I love her till I die."
—"There's a Lady Sweet and Kind," Thomas Ford,
sixteenth-century English poet

$\mathcal{N}$o one knows who inspired this much-quoted verse. She may have been young or perhaps a woman of age. She could have been a milkmaid. She could have been a princess. But one thing is for sure, she had charisma, magnetism, and a certain *je ne sais quoi*; that special something beyond looks that makes a woman unforgettable and ageless. We have all run into a woman who, whenever she walks through the door, simply owns the room. She exudes grace and charm. The light in her eyes and the pureness of her smile make her seem approachable yet unattainable. She's confident and moves with an effortless grace. Although slightly intimidating, she's sexy, elegant, and completely captivating. We wonder what it must be like to be her.

What does she have that I don't? In your mind, she may not be the most beautiful woman at the party, or the most stylish, yet she remains completely unforgettable. Why?

For more than two decades, amazing women have approached me for my take on beauty, style, body image, and the true meaning of success. When I think about their questions, I realize we all want to develop the traits that make us "that woman." But what is it about "that woman" that draws people like moths to a flame? It is something almost indefinable.

Since my early modeling days, I have been intrigued by the qualities and attributes that make one person more desirable and more appealing than another. I've seen exquisite, trendy girls who have plenty of "it" squander their beauty and potential by behaving cheaply and obsessing purely on how they look on the outside. I've also watched "plain Janes" grow into beautiful women and timid boys become confident, strong, handsome young men (some of these men and women have contributed their insight and advice throughout these pages).

Throughout my career, I have gained a perspective from both my personal and professional life. I have been all over the world and met all kinds of people. I have come to realize that we all fight with the same issues, the same insecurities. And we are all fighting to be unforgettable. They say the pen is mightier than the sword, so with pen in hand, come on this journey with me to an Unforgettable You.

XOXO,

Daisy

Unforgettable You

Chapter One

Who Are You? Baby, Who Are You?

Knowing Who You Are

"You have come here to find
what you already have."
—Buddhist aphorism

I'M FROM JERSEY. And when I was seventeen, I thought that I could not ask for more out of life than *big* hair, bright nails, Camaros, shopping malls, attitudes, and accents. And then one day, my world shifted slightly and forever.

My next-door neighbor worked for Piero Dimitri, a couture Italian designer. They needed someone to fill in last-minute at a photo shoot. Without realizing what I was getting myself into, I headed into the city with my neighbor. I thought it was a one-shot deal, but it became a regular gig, and then I became Piero's "fit model." (The fit model is used to fit the samples on as they are being made. Back in the eighties, fit models were taller and curvier, but later Kate Moss became everyone's fit model, and I was no longer easily fitting into sample sizes. Fortunately for me the TV world came calling before that became a problem.

After I'd been working for Piero for a few months, he suggested that I take on more jobs and get an agent. This is when I started to really see the world outside of Jersey. I would take the PATH train into the city, and in ten minutes I was ten miles away and ten years ahead of anything comfortable or familiar.

All of the other girls came from other countries. They had their own apartments. They flat-ironed their hair. Their nails were short and barely polished. Their clothes were black and boring and could have used some kick-ass accessories. But mostly, their hair was in dire, dire need of some serious back-combing and hairspray.

And then there was me.

One day, Piero asked me to stand in front of a full-length mirror in his studio. "Daisy, look. Look at yourself." I had my big Jersey hair, my fluorescent painted nails, a wider-than-wide white belt over my dress, chunky accessories. I thought I looked pretty damn fabulous. "What is the first thing you notice?" Piero asked me.

"Well, my belt, I guess."

"Exactly. And what's the next thing?"

"My nails? My hair?"

"Exactly. Exactly."

I stared at him. Was he trying to make a point?

"Darling, why would you want people to notice your belt, your hair, your nails, before they notice your face?"

> *"Live as if you were to die tomorrow. Learn as if you were to live forever."*
>
> —*Gandhi*

This was the first of many valuable pieces of advice that I would respectfully ignore. When I was seventeen, I thought I knew it all. In fact, I thought I knew it all until I was about twenty-five. Until I was about thirty. OK, until about right now. The truth is, I'll never know it all. I will always be on a journey of rediscovery. Once I realized this, my path to discovery truly began.

Unforgettable Tip:
Only a fool knows everything.

Unforgettable You

The purpose of this book is to help you become a more aware, enhanced, happier version of yourself. I have spent the last twenty years of my life learning about myself (mostly the hard way), and I still have the nerve to

Unforgettable Tip:

Be yourself, but always be willing to be a better version of yourself.

continue to evolve and change. When I was younger, I was so stubbornly trying to "be myself" that I never stopped to find out who I really was and who I really wanted to be. I hope that this book inspires you to take the time to discover who you are, no matter what age you may be. I only really began to discover who I was when I was in my thirties, but, my God, I wish I had started earlier. I could have been dan-ger-ous. This is the book that *I've* been looking for since I was twenty.

"After all these years, I am still involved in the process of self-discovery. It's better to explore life and make mistakes than to play it safe. Mistakes are part of the dues one pays for a full life."

—Sophia Loren

My first modeling card, 1985.

Let's Begin at the Beginning

I had been working as a model for a few years when I was offered a job as weather girl for Univision. I knew nothing about the weather, but I knew how to speak Spanish, and I could read a teleprompter. I figured I would give it a shot. I did not really stop to think about what I was getting myself into. Meteorology. Satellite weather maps. Live television. *Live* television! Did I mention it was live TV? What was I thinking? I wasn't, thank God. I just went for it. I think the station executives stayed interested in me because I just wasn't fazed by any of it. No matter what challenge they threw at me, I would tackle it as though I'd been doing it for years. I was giving it my all, but I wasn't obsessing over every little thing. I learned from my mistakes, I listened to advice, and, most important, I was having a good time. I was having fun, and I *really* loved that my parents were proud of me. During my school years, my grades were terribly average; I was enjoying the newfound glory of doing something I was good at and came naturally to me. That said, I knew I did not want to be doing weather for the rest of my life. Yet at this point, I still didn't know what I wanted to do. I certainly didn't think this TV thing would last.

I would come home and sit on my parents' couch and watch MTV. I loved to watch the original veejays, and I would envision myself as one of them. I could really see myself on TV, interviewing the world's biggest stars, traveling to the hottest hot spots, being invited to the best parties. "That is my dream job," I told my mom.

"Well, send them a tape," Mom said.

"That's not how it works," I informed her (remember, I knew it all back then). "You have to have a big agent, get an audition. All that stuff." Remember, this was before reality shows—the only way to get the job was to audition and interview for it.

"Just send them a tape."

I still thought she was wrong, but I put together a tape anyway. My friend at the station helped me to splice together some of my weather pieces, and we sent off the tape. At this time, MTV did not have a Spanish division, but footage of my Spanish weather forecast was all I had. I sent it, then tried to forget about it. Somewhere, in an MTV office, Steve Leeds (the on-air talent director) received a tape of some chick doing the weather in Spanish. He later told me that he didn't understand a word of it, but he thought I was cute enough, so he stashed it under his desk. He forgot about it until eight months later, when another MTV exec told him they had been interviewing hundreds of girls, looking for someone to host the one-hour Latin MTV program they were launching. They couldn't find anyone who fit the bill. He pulled out my tape, and out of nowhere, I got a call for an audition.

Oh, that audition. It was not my finest hour.

I was so nervous that I woke up early, giving myself about six hours just to get ready. And my eye was swollen shut from some sort of insect bite I'd gotten while I was asleep. *That's it,* I told myself, *I'm not going. It's just not meant to be.* But for three hours, I iced my eye and put on every cream in the medicine cabinet. I did a bunch of makeup tricks, made my hair *big,* and then flipped some of the hair over to cover most of the damage. After a few hours and lots of makeup, my eye didn't look terrible. Oh, and I also took Benadryl (perhaps not the wisest decision).

I then got dressed in (are you ready for it?) a white leather miniskirt, a white leather-fringed jacket, and white leather boots. Also fringed. (See the picture. This was in at the time, I swear.) I got on the PATH train, and by the time I reached the city, there was a sleeting ice storm. I could not get a cab anywhere, so I had to walk to the studio. I arrived forty-five minutes late, and I was a mess. My hair

Proudly showing off the fierce white leather outfit
I wore on my first MTV audition.

was flattened down, I was covered in disgusting New York
City sleet, and I was doped up on Benadryl.

When I walked into that studio, I was sure I was never getting the job, so I just went for it. I played to the camera, I tried not to be nervous, and I set myself at ease. My executive producer, Barbara Corcoran, later told me that this is what saved me: "You looked like a mess when you walked in, but once you got on camera, you lit up." If it had not been for my weather gig (which, if I'm being honest, was not my dream job), I would not have had the experience in front of the camera or the comfort level to get through that audition. This is why I am a true believer in giving it my all, no matter what I am doing. There is a purpose for everything, even if it doesn't quite make sense at the moment. In life, seemingly insignificant "gigs" are exactly what prepare you for "the dream job."

Unforgettable Tip:
Whatever you do, no matter how trivial or how fabulously important, do it with integrity, dignity, and style.

Still, when I walked out of that building (my hair fully flattened and stuck together now, the gray sleet stained into all that white leather), I was certain that I was going back to reading weather maps for a few more months. There was a lot yet to learn. And then, of course, the impossible happened. MTV called me the next day and told me I had the job. And that's when everything really changed.

I stepped into a world of celebrity and fame and parties that I never knew actually existed. And I found out quickly that there was a lot to learn. There were fancy dinners with seventeen pieces of silverware and cocktail parties with the most glamorous of the glamorous. I was mingling with the world's biggest rock stars, making small talk with newsmakers, and rubbing elbows with top supermodels. I was in over my head.

The whole "it" crowd was fascinating to me (still is), but I was always particularly intrigued by a certain type of woman who really stood out. At every party, there was one woman who possessed a beauty and elegance that set her apart from the crowd. Sometimes she was a rock-and-roll chick or maybe a high-society lady, sometimes she was a downtown girl clad in vintage, and other times she was a perfectly polished uptown gal. These standouts were all unique, but they had certain traits in common: presence, grace, elegance, style, and inner tranquility. They knew who they were. They were secure, sure of themselves, and they had an opinion.

I was sure of one thing: I wanted to be like these women.

"Always act as though you are wearing an invisible crown."

—*Unknown*

At this time, I was young and impressionable. Everyone was saying, "Dare to be different" and that old cliché "Be yourself." Sure, we were all being ourselves, but we had no idea who the hell we really were because we were mostly imitating each other. We still had so much to learn. The first lesson was not to take the "Be yourself" credo too seriously. Always leave some room to grow and improve who you are, because the road to self-discovery should never end.

Unforgettable Tip:
Before you can "be yourself," you must find out who you really are.

We must all take the time to get to know ourselves. What do you like? What do you dislike? In my early twenties, I was constantly surround by people who had so much—so much fame, money, notoriety, experience, class, and so on. I was intimidated at first. To be honest, everyone was giving me advice about what to do, how to act, who to be. And in return, I was giving advice on everything. I gave advice (or dictated) to my parents, to my sister, to my friends. We were a bunch of young people dishing out advice about things we knew nothing about. Everybody thought they had the secret to success,

Unforgettable Tip:
You can "be yourself" and still work on yourself at the same time.

including me. As time passed, I learned to smile politely and take only the advice that I truly admired and that made

"Opinions are like assholes. Everybody's got one."
—New Jersey aphorism

sense to me. I also learned to keep some of those unsolic-
ited opinions to myself (I do wish I'd learned that sooner).

I discovered that I was most inspired by those who
managed to maintain their individuality, self-respect, and
dignity. By observing, I discovered that "being myself"
meant taking inspiration from these men and women but
never imitating them. The truth is, nobody's perfect. Also,
I realized early on that if you try to imitate the rock-and-
roll chick, the high-society woman, the downtown girl,
and the uptown lady, you end up a hot, schizophrenic
mess.

The mistake we all make in our youth is adopting others' points of view without really thinking, *Is this my point
of view?* It is so important to self-evaluate and ask ourselves who we are so that we are not constantly adopting
the style and opinions of others. Popular opinion does not
automatically make it *your* opinion.

To know yourself fully, you have to question yourself.

Throughout this book, there will be several questionnaires. Some I have made up, some I have pulled from other places. Let's start with my very favorite, the Proust Questionnaire. It was a game that French novelist Marcel Proust made famous as a parlor game. Proust believed that by answering these questions, we reveal our true selves.

Unforgettable Tip:
Ask yourself questions.

I found a coffee-table book with blank Proust Questionnaires. I keep this book in my guest room and love to have our friends and family answer the questionnaire. These questions were really meant for fun, yet I found that answering them wasn't as easy as I thought it would be. I really wanted whoever read my page to know about me. Part of me was trying to be honest, and part of me was trying to be cool. I realized that when my "cool" answer was also my honest answer, I was solid in that area. When my "cool" answer was not completely honest, that was an area I had to work on and explore.

"Find out who you are, and do it on purpose."
—Dolly Parton

Your Proust Questionnaire

1. What is your idea of perfect happiness?

_____

_____

_____

_____

_____

2. What is your greatest fear?

_____

_____

_____

_____

_____

3. What is the trait you most deplore in yourself?

_____

_____

_____

_____

_____

4. What is the trait you most deplore in others?

_____

_____

_____

_____

_____

5. Which living person do you most admire?

_____

_____

_____

_____

_____

6. What is your greatest extravagance?

_____

_____

_____

_____

_____

7. What is your current state of mind?

_____

_____

_____

_____

_____

8. What do you consider the most overrated virtue?

_____

_____

_____

_____

_____

9. On what occasion do you lie?

_____

_____

_____

_____

_____

10. What do you most dislike about your appearance?

_____

_____

_____

_____

_____

11. Which living person do you most despise?

_____

_____

_____

_____

_____

12. What is the quality you most like in a man?

_____

_____

_____

_____

_____

13. What is the quality you most like in a woman?

_____

_____

_____

_____

_____

14. Which words or phrases do you most overuse?

_____

_____

_____

_____

_____

15. What or who is the greatest love of your life?

_____

_____

_____

_____

_____

16. When and where were you happiest?

_____

_____

_____

_____

_____

17. Which talent would you most like to have?

_____

_____

_____

_____

_____

18. If you could change one thing about yourself, what would it be?

_____

_____

_____

_____

_____

19. What do you consider your greatest achievement?

_____

_____

_____

_____

_____

20. If you were to die and come back as a person or a thing, what would it be?

_____

_____

_____

_____

_____

21. Where would you most like to live?

_____

_____

_____

_____

_____

22. What is your most treasured possession?

_____

_____

_____

_____

_____

23. What do you regard as the lowest depth of misery?

_____

_____

_____

_____

_____

24. What is your favorite occupation?

_____

_____

_____

_____

_____

25. What is your most marked characteristic?

_____

_____

_____

_____

_____

26. What do you most value in your friends?

_____

_____

_____

_____

27. Who are your favorite writers?

_____

_____

_____

_____

28. Who is your hero of fiction?

_____

_____

_____

_____

_____

29. Which historical figure do you most identify with?

_____

_____

_____

_____

_____

30. Who are your heroes in real life?

_____

_____

_____

_____

_____

31. What are your favorite names?

_____

_____

_____

_____

_____

32. What is it that you most dislike?

_____

_____

_____

_____

_____

33. What is your greatest regret?

_____

_____

_____

_____

_____

34. How would you like to die?

_____

_____

_____

_____

_____

35. What is your motto?

_____

_____

_____

_____

_____

"The real voyage of discovery consists not in seeking new lands, but in seeing with new eyes."
—Marcel Proust

One Unforgettable Woman

Cleopatra

"Be it known that we, the greatest, are misthought."

From her makeup to her jewels to her serious powers of seduction (she hooked both Marc Antony and Julius Caesar), Cleopatra is one of our earliest examples of a kick-ass confident woman. Legend has it that she had the sails of her ship soaked in jasmine oils. When she would set off to war or to meet with her lover, Marc Antony, her fragrance would blow across the shores, and the people would line the coast to witness her arrival. The chick knew how to make an entrance.

Unforgettable Tip:
Never be ordinary.

TAKE NOTE: *Unforgettable You* is meant

to be a springboard for you to discover who you are and who you want to be. Now that you have answered the Proust Questionnaire, take a bit more time to ask yourself who you are and what you really love and value.

Who am I?

     I am . . .

_____

_____

_____

_____

_____

_____

_____

_____

_____

_____

sign here

Who am I?

I am . . .

a blessed being. A woman, a daughter, a sister, an aunt, a faithful lover and friend. I am
strong, independent, loyal, caring, and loving. I'm
usually happy but sometimes grumpy. I'm usually
honest. I have good instincts. I'm a good judge
of character. I'm feminine but a bit rough
around the edges. I have many things in common
with most girls, but I'm not ordinary. I am the
one you can count on, depend on, trust...and the
one you don't want to cross. I live in the present. I love my life and the people in it. I am myself but always trying to be a better version of
myself.

Daisy

sign here

This is who I am.

TAKE NOTE: *What Do You Love?* Use this page to make a list of your very favorite things. This will help you to realize what you truly value. Many times we let ourselves be consumed by our jobs, our ex-boyfriends, the last ten pounds that won't come off, the guy who won't call, and so on. But once you see written down on paper the things that you truly value, you can remind yourself to focus on these items, make time for them, and cultivate them. Does that guy who won't call make the list?

A few of your favorite things:

_____

_____

_____

_____

_____

_____

Raindrops on roses . . .

And whiskers on kittens . . .

A few of my favorite things . . .

My dogs and my family

Pizza

Long hikes

Scotch

Lazy mornings

Incense and candles

Finding a bargain

Splurging on those I love

Learning about other people's passions

Nature

Quiet

Bossa nova

Cheese

The moon

Animals

Fashion

Everything I love.

A great makeover/under

Being informal

Pop culture

My career/brand

Giving my time and money to what I believe in

Massages

Family traditions

Indian food

Bon Jovi

Proper afternoon tea

Spending weekends on the boat with my
    family

Fabulous family holidays

Snowboarding in Aspen

Snuggling with my dogs

Bright copper kettles . . .

And warm woolen mittens . . .

Since I am always interested in what other people love, I had a few of my friends make their own lists (have your friends do this too. It will surprise you and help you really get to know them better). Here are a few of my friends' favorite things:

The Godfather and Sonny Corleone

The Giants and the Yankees

Garlic and oil

The beach

Espresso

The smell of very old books

Used bookstores

Cross necklaces

Jesus' abs

High ponytails

White wife-beaters

NY Pretzel smell

Ketchup on my salad

Artichokes

Grill marks on my food

Sundays

The 60 Minutes watch

The Wonder Years

Southern accents

Bon Jovi

Bruce Springsteen

Joni Mitchell

'80s music

Guys with glasses

Men's white shirts

Flip-flops

The smell of fall and spring

Summer

The Jersey shore

Miami

Long night runs

Escarole soup

My mom's smell

My dad's phone manner

I have only recently started to carry a journal with me. I wish I'd had it earlier. I still have to remind myself to jot down my thoughts, but when I look back on what I have written, it really helps me put life in perspective. I keep my list of favorite things, things I am thankful for, and my "Who am I" paragraph at the front of my journal. I am constantly adding to these pages. Throughout my journal, I am also continually asking myself questions. Do not edit yourself in your journal. The whole point of a journal is to be open. Don't play it safe, don't try to be profound, and don't worry about anybody finding it. And so, in the interest of practicing what I preach, I'll share a few of my favorite pages from my journal with you:

> *Unforgettable Tip:*
> Buy a journal. There is no better self-discovery tool.

Brown paper packages . . .

         Tied up with string . . .

MY JOURNAL

What makes a woman unforgettable?

Confidence

Strength

Dignity

Kindness

An air of mystery/privacy

What makes a woman unattractive?

Self-consciousness

Being loud

Being promiscuous/easy/desperate

Acting needy/dependent

Being obsessive/compulsive

Nagging

Things I know now know that I wish I knew
when I was twenty:

I wish I knew my potential.

I wish I knew how to use youth to my advantage.

I wish I knew more about the world and people.

I wish I was more stylish or that I individualized
my style more.

I wish I paid more attention to everything.

I wish I'd known I'd fall in love more than
once . . . and with different intensity.

I wish I knew how lucky I was.

I wish I knew sometimes I wasn't being very
nice.

I wish I'd known who really had my back.

I wish I'd been more spiritual.

I wish I'd learned the importance of forgiveness.

I remember at one party, a fabulous model came up to me. I had been sipping champagne and been turning the glass, so that I had given myself a rather unattractive line of red lipstick on the bridge of my nose. "Darling," she told me very sweetly, "let me give you a tip. When you are drinking champagne, always drink out of the same spot so that you don't get that line of lipstick on your nose."

Wow, I thought, *she's a goddamn genius!* And that's when I realized that I could learn a lot by observing. And I guess I was observing when I didn't even realize it.

Unforgettable Tip:
Take a genuine interest in others.

I have always been a people watcher. I can sit at a café and watch the people for hours—human actions and behaviors fascinate me. There is so much to learn about how you want to be and how you do not want to be by just sitting back and taking in the world.

I love to watch the way people talk to each other, the way they carry themselves, their body language, their tone. It is one of my favorite things to do on a lazy afternoon, and I am still somewhat surprised to discover that I too, am being watched. The first time I noticed a table of people staring at me and whispering, I was a little freaked out. Yet I also completely understood their intrigue. It made me more aware of how I act in public. I try to be confident and sure of myself but not self-conscious. I remind myself to keep my cool and be courteous when someone upsets me and makes me want to "go Jersey" on them.

But whether or not you are in the public eye, it is helpful to remember that there's always somebody watching you. A few years ago, I was shopping, zoned out in my little world of retail therapy. I had been in the store for about an hour, and when I reached the checkout, the cashier said, "It is so great to have you in the store. I am such a fan of yours." Then she leaned in and told me, "And all the security guys in the back, they are so excited. They have had the cameras zoomed in on you the whole time you were here." I thought, *Shit! Did I pick my nose? Did I pull my wedgie? I hope I didn't embarrass myself.* After that day, I have tried to remind myself that there may always be a group of security guys watching me. They may be watching you, too. Kenneth Cole once ran an ad campaign with billboards that read: "You are on video-camera an average of 10 times a day, are you dressed for it?" More important, are you acting for it? What would you say if you saw yourself on playback? What would your mother say? Would you be embarrassed or proud of what you saw?

TAKE NOTE: *What I Know for Sure*

What I know for sure . . . about who I am.

The late film critic Gene Siskel used to ask in his interviews, "What do you know for sure?" The first time he asked Oprah Winfrey, she didn't know how to answer. Now, in the back of every *O Magazine*, Oprah writes a column entitled "What I Know for Sure." I think it is a genius question on Gene's part and a genius column on Oprah's part. I decided to start making my own "What I know for sure" lists, and I have included them at the end of each chapter. After my list, I encourage you to create your own "What I know for sure" page.

What I know for sure about . . . myself:

I'm kind.

I'm not perfect.

I'm thankful.

I'm privileged.

I'm lucky.

I'm resilient.

I'm generous.

I'm loved.

I love dogs.

I'm not very disciplined.

I believe in karma.

Your Turn

Now it is your turn to write down what you know for sure about yourself. Use this list to help you become aware of who you really are (flaws and all). Only include items that you know about yourself for sure right now, not things you wish were true or hope will be true someday. Be honest, and put all your cards on the table. You have to let people know who they are playing with, so no bluffing. Write a date below your list, and come back to it in a year and revise.

What I know for sure about . . . myself:

_____

_____

_____

_____

_____

_____

_____

_____

_____

_____

_____

_____

Chapter Two

• • • • • • • • • • • • •

Just Like a Woman

Grace, Elegance, and Etiquette

"Elegance is refusal."
—Coco Chanel

*O*NCE UPON A time, there were women named Audrey Hepburn, Grace Kelly, Jacqueline Kennedy. They never aired their dirty laundry. They always stepped out of the car properly (and I'm pretty sure they always wore underwear). They always dressed appropriately and some-times stylishly fierce. They were ladies, and they were dis-creet. They knew how to walk the fine line between having fun and acting foolish.

I look around at some of the starlets of today, and I wonder, where have all the ladies gone? It seems we are experiencing a gender switch. Young girls are behaving like dudes (and badly behaved dudes at that). From the booze to the drugs, the sex tapes to the jail time, the laun-dry list of sexual partners to the lack of underwear—this is the example that Hollywood is setting for our young girls.

Or does this represent what is going on in society? I'm not sure.

When did our culture become so accepting of this "Girls Gone Wild" behavior? I'm all for girl power, but some of these girls are giving the rest of us a bad name. I believe you can be a "take no shit," strong, powerful, successful, liberated woman and still be a lady. In fact, I think there's nothing sexier. Men and women are equal, but we are definitely not the same. I'm not saying these ridiculous, embarrassing displays of stupidity are acceptable in guys. They are certainly not. Yet I have to say that it is much worse when girls behave so crudely. We are prettier, classier, and softer than that. We can achieve so much more when we respect ourselves.

I've seen women at parties getting drunk out of their skulls, dancing like strippers, cursing like sailors, making moves on numerous men (and women), and just being plain loud and obnoxious. They think they are the life of the party. In reality, people are embarrassed for them. I know I am. These women are just showing how insecure they are. Men may want to spend fifteen minutes with them (you know what I mean), but they are not going to take them seriously (at least, not the men I'd be interested in). And they sure aren't going to "put a ring on it."

Don't get me wrong. I'm not a prude. I enjoy having a drink at a gathering, having a good laugh with friends at a party, and flirting a bit. And in the company of good friends and good wine, my language gets pretty colorful (you can take the girl outta Jersey . . .). But there's an art to being a lady, and it is a learned art. It is through practice, time, education, and observation that a girl transforms herself. We start to learn how to become a lady when we are about four, so it's important to remind ourselves of those early lessons.

Lessons I learned when I was four . . .
that I still live by at forty

- Keep your mouth shut when someone else is speaking.
- Stop fidgeting.
- Keep your voice down.
- Wait your turn.
- Share.
- Don't talk with your mouth full.
- Respect your elders.
- Don't run with sharp objects.
- Don't be a tattle-tale.
- Don't be a nag.
- Stop whining.
- Say you're sorry.
- Look at people when they are talking to you.

- Sit up straight.

- Clean up your own messes.

- Be nice.

- Say thank you.

- Don't lift your dress above your head.

My parents and I in Madrid, 1970.

"*The best way to learn to be a lady is to see how other ladies do it.*"
—Mae West

What Is Etiquette?

It is sending thank you notes, never showing up to a home empty-handed, and respecting your elders. It is never speaking with your mouth full, realizing when to keep your mouth shut, and knowing when to bite your tongue. A woman with etiquette understands all of the little details that make a big impression. It is not as hard as you think. It requires a little bit of work and a small investment in a great etiquette manual. My favorites:

Emily Post's Etiquette, by Peggy Post. This is the etiquette bible, now in its seventeenth edition.

Emily Post on Etiquette, by Elizabeth L. Post. A condensed, pocket-sized version of Emily Post's advice. This can be carried around in your purse and referred to (discreetly) when you have no clue what to do in a social situation.

Tiffany's Table Manners for Teenagers. A classic from 1961 that every girl, young and old, should have.

The Emily Vanderbilt Complete Book of Etiquette, by Nancy Tuckerman and Nancy Dunnan. An authoritative book on etiquette. It was first published in 1952 and has been updated for the modern woman.

Each of these books go into the thorough details of etiquette. Don't be overwhelmed. The more you know, the easier it gets. I'll start you out with the Cliffs Notes of what every lady must know.

Table Manners 101

I am always shocked at how few people really know their table manners. Come on, it's not rocket science. When you sit down at a proper dinner table, there are rules every lady (and gentleman) must know:

- Put the napkin on your lap right away.

- Wait until everyone is served before you start eating.

- Don't freak out if there are seventeen pieces of silverware; just move from outside in.

- Your bread plate is on your left, drink is on your right.

- If in doubt, wait for somebody else to make a move, and then follow his or her lead.

- Never speak with your mouth full. Not even half full, thank you.

- If you are choking, remove yourself from the table. Nobody else needs to see that. Unless you're going to die. Then, by all means, ask someone for help.

How to set a table, the cheat sheet:

- The napkin goes to the left of the plate, along with the fork or forks. If you are using more than one fork, the larger one sits closer to the plate.

- The knife and spoon go on the right. The knife sits closest to the plate, and the blade should always face the plate.

- Place the water and wineglasses at the top right of the plate.

- Place the bread plate to the top left.

How to Be a Modern Lady 101

My friends used to ask me the fun questions. What does Jon Bon Jovi look like up close? What does Bill Clinton smell like? But now, when we sit around or gab on the phone, my friends will say, "Well, what *is* the right way to step out of a car?" Or "I'm in the waiting room. Should I not be talking on the phone?" Or "She asked me when I was going to have kids. What the hell do you say to that?" Does this mean we're getting older? Nah, it just means we're becoming more mature and more aware. Lately, I have taken to writing down some notes from conversations I've had with friends or even with strangers at dinner parties. I realize that there are some common social hurdles that the modern girl is faced with, and I tried to compile a hit list of the questions and answers that always seem to surface.

What is the proper way to step out of a car?

Most of us don't have a camera shooting up at us every time we step out of a car; however, most of the time, somebody is watching us. When stepping out of the car, remember to keep it elegant. If you are wearing a dress, it can be a bit tricky. Slowly, keep your knees together, be graceful, and, for God's sake, wear underwear! If your dress is so sheer or so tight that you can't possibly wear one of the seventeen million thong/stocking/Spanx options available to you, then you should probably not wear that dress.

What is the best way to deflect a rude question?

I've had my share of rude questions, and I've come to realize that sometimes people don't even know when they are being rude. We should always be prepared to stay calm, not get too offended, and move on. I find it is always helpful to have a few key responses ready, just in case:

- "Oh, well, that caught me off guard. I'll have to think about that for a minute. Did you try the shrimp cocktail? Delicious."

- "Oh, I have enough to think about without worrying about other people's problems."

- "That's a very flattering dress. Is that new?"

When it's just a plain rude question or comment ("When are you going to have a baby—you're not getting any younger," or "Isn't it about time you get married?" or "How much did you pay for that?" or "Is he a good lover?" or "I'm so glad you guys broke up; I always thought he was such a jerk"), sometimes the only answer is:

- "Well, that's not really anyone's business."

- "That's inappropriate."

Of course, always smile politely (and a bit sarcastically) when you are forced to whip these babies out.

How do you politely remove yourself from a conversation?

- "Excuse me, I think I just saw an old friend."

- "Excuse me, I need to powder my nose."

- "Please excuse me for just a moment."
- Don't wait for a response, just smile and walk away.

What's the rule now, two kisses on the cheek or one?

I tend to do what I'm used to, which is one kiss (it's also easier). But I don't want to leave anyone hanging. Plus, half my family is from Spain, so they kiss twice. Don't anticipate it, just slowly go with the flow. If there are others saying hello or good-bye, just do what they do. When kissing a man, he should be initiating the kiss and do most of the leaning anyway.

What is a rule of thumb for drinking at a formal party or dinner?

It's sexy to be able to sip one or two glasses of wine slowly throughout the night. It's not a drinking contest. Drunk is never sexy. If someone is insisting on filling your glass, when you're done drinking, simply say "No, thank you." If they insist, let them fill it, and say thanks. But remember, just because it's there doesn't mean you have to drink it. So, don't.

What is a good time to arrive at a party?

If the invite says eight for a party, I'd show up by nine. Unless it is a sit-down dinner party, in this case, remember they can't start without you. Show up around 8:15. No later than 8:30. I never want to be the first one there and never the last to leave.

Cell Phone Etiquette 101

I could write an entire book on this. It would include all of the inappropriate (and amusing) conversations I have heard over the years. But for right now, I'll keep it to a few pages.

Where and when should you avoid answering a call?

It's really become the norm to be on the phone talking or texting, no matter what else you're doing or whom you're doing it with. I think it's rude. If you spend most of our dinner talking or texting someone else, why did you agree to have dinner with me and not the other person? It seems as if common sense and common courtesy don't apply to mobile phones. Well, be advised, it most certainly does.

Cell phone etiquette really depends on your lifestyle and your job. If you're an assistant (especially my assistant) or a coordinator or you have a job or business where it *is* your job to be on the phone, then, by all means, discreetly pay attention to that phone. But let's face it, unless you're a doctor on call, you probably don't have to be available 24/7. If you're at a business meeting, you should turn the ringer off and let the call go to voice mail. Return the calls when you have privacy and time to talk. Unless it's an important business call or an emergency, and you just have to take that call. In that case, you should say something like "I really apologize, but I must answer this call, excuse me," and excuse yourself right out of the room. Never take a call during a meeting, lunch, or dinner in front of everyone where all can hear you. Not everyone needs or wants to hear your business.

It takes an independent person with self-confidence and control of his or her life to make the choice not to take a call. Some might think it makes them look "popular" if they're always on phone. Believe it or not, you seem more important if you are picky about who gets to talk with you and when than if you talk to anyone, anytime. If you have to take every single call, all the time, you come off as needy, insecure, codependant, and always available to everyone about anything. There is nothing sexy about that. You have to schedule and control your life. You must use common sense regarding what calls need to be answered right now and what can wait a half-hour. Generally speaking, whatever you're doing at the time and whomever you're doing it with should be your priority at that moment. Remember, there was a time when we didn't carry a mobile phone everywhere and we'd have to wait to get home or call our answering machines. And you know what? The world didn't fall apart.

Is it ever OK to answer the phone (or text or e-mail) at the table?

Yes, if you have children, if you're a doctor, or if you're Batman. And if you must take the call or send a text, apologize and excuse yourself from the table.

What is a polite way to end a call?

You don't have to wait until the other person is ready to hang up. You can always say, "I'm sorry, I'm just in the middle of something. I'll call you back later," or "Sorry, I have to run. May I get back to you?" If the person insists by asking, "Oh, what are you doing?" (don't be the one asking that, by the way), just say, "I'll explain later, gotta run. 'Bye!" People will learn to respect your time.

SIX CELL RULES

1. Keep your voice down. We can all hear you, even if the person on the other end can't.

2. Keep personal conversations private. Don't talk about that itchy rash and that bastard you think gave it to you, as you walk down the supermarket aisles. They're not walls, they're aisles, and we can hear you.

3. Just because you can have "I'm too sexy for my shirt, so sexy it hurts" as a ringtone doesn't mean you should. Let people get to know you a little before they discover you have dreadful taste in music. Loud musical ringtones usually scare the crap out of people when they come out of nowhere, and they're definitely not professional. If you're over twenty-one, you should probably stick to something more grown-up and classy like an actual ring or a soft bell or something discreet.

4. At the movies, put it away, and put it on silent. We can hear and feel it vibrate, and yes, we can see the bright light when you're texting, and yes it's distracting and annoying.

5. I don't care if you *are* Danica Patrick, no, you can't text and drive.

6. Don't talk full-blown business in public. When you give actual figures and talk numbers or deal breakers in line at the bank or on the plane where everyone can hear you, you just sound like an asshole.

"Eliza, you are to stay here for the next six months learning to speak beautifully, like a lady in a florist's shop. If you work hard and do as you're told, you shall sleep in a proper bedroom, have lots to eat, and money to buy chocolates and go for rides in taxis. But if you are naughty and idle, you shall sleep in the back kitchen amongst the black beetles, and be walloped by Mrs. Pearce with a broomstick. At the end of six months you will be taken to Buckingham Palace, in a carriage, beautifully dressed. If the king finds out you are not a lady, you will be taken to the Tower of London, where your head will be cut off as a warning to other presumptuous flower girls!"

—My Fair Lady

Watching How It's Done

Classic movies teach us some of the most basic elements of elegance. And most of them show us how a formerly ill-mannered young girl is transformed into a graceful young lady (ever get the feeling they're trying to tell you something?). Here are a few of my favorites:

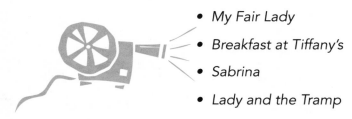

- *My Fair Lady*
- *Breakfast at Tiffany's*
- *Sabrina*
- *Lady and the Tramp*

Every Woman Should

Glamour writer Pamela Redmond Satran once compiled a list of items every woman should have and what she should know. I loved it the first time I saw it, and it inspired me to make my own set of "Every Woman Should" lists.

Every Woman Should Know:

- Her social security number.
- The names of the current president, vice president, and secretary of state.
- The daily headlines from the local paper or a major national paper (I love *USA Today*).

- Her favorite book, movie, and band.
- The current number one bestseller (and what it's about).
- How to play at least one sport.
- The name of her favorite restaurant.
- What fashion trends don't work for her.
- What makes her happy.
- How to mind her P's and Q's.

MIND YOUR P'S AND Q'S: GRAMMAR RULES EVERY GIRL MUST KNOW

Well vs. Good

Oftentimes I hear people use *well* instead of *good,* because they think *well* sounds more proper. Not true! A smart lady knows when to use *well* and when to use *good.*

Good is an adjective, used to describe a noun or pronoun.

The cake is good.

School was good.

Well is an adverb, used to describe a verb.

> I am doing well, thank you.
>
> The meeting went well.
>
> I ran well.

Me vs. I

The same goes for *me* and *I*. Many people think that *I* sounds correct in all situations, but educated women know differently.

> *I* is always the subject of the verb (*I cooked dinner*).
>
> *Me* is a always the object of the verb (*Come to the beach with me*).

Easy enough. The confusion comes when we add another person to the mix. *(Steve and I cooked dinner. Come to the beach with Sandra and me.)* The easiest way to tell if you should use *I* or *me* in these sentences is to take away the other noun and see if it still makes sense.

Examples:

- *Rosana and I went shopping. I went shopping.* (Yes.)
- *Rosana and me went shopping. Me went shopping.* (Hell no.)

- *Mom was talking about you and me. Mom was talking about me.* (Yes.)
- *Mom was talking about you and I. Mom was talking about I.* (Hell no.)

Words a Lady Always Knows, No Matter Where She Goes

English	Hello	Good-bye	Thank You
Spanish	Hola	Adios	Gracias
French	Bonjour	Au revoir	Merci
German	Hallo	Auf wiedersehen	Danke
Italian	Ciao	Ciao	Grazie
Japanese	Konnichiwa	Sayonara	Arigato

Every Woman Should Know How To:

- Do her own laundry.
- Change a tire.
- Clean the house (including the toilet).
- Use chopsticks.

- Balance a checkbook.

- Put on fake eyelashes.

- Blow-dry her hair.

- Mix a kick-ass cocktail.

- Give a compliment.

- Take a compliment.

- Write a great thank-you note.

- Dance.

- Be alone.

- Be quiet.

- Play a proper game (poker, chess, backgammon).

- Make at least two good meals (one for a dinner party, one for comfort food).

My Favorite Comfort Food Recipe: Mac and Cheese

It ain't good for you, but it's good as all hell.

Ingredients

1 pound pasta

Salt

3 tablespoons butter

3 tablespoons all-purpose flour

2 cups whole milk

½ cup half-and-half

8 ounces shredded sharp cheddar

8 ounces shredded mozzarella

4 ounces grated parmesan

Black pepper

For the topping:

1 cup coarse bread crumbs

1 tablespoon butter, melted

2 tablespoons chopped fresh parsley

Crispy pancetta (optional)

Salt

Cook pasta until al dente in a large pot of boiling salted water. Drain.

Meanwhile, in a large saucepan, melt the butter over medium heat. Add the flour and stir to form a smooth paste. Cook for about 2 minutes, being careful not to let it brown. Gradually add the milk and the half-and-half, and simmer until thickened slightly, stirring continuously. Remove from the heat. Stir in the three cheeses, and season with black pepper to taste. Add the cooked pasta, and mix into the cheese sauce thoroughly.

Preheat oven to 400 degrees F.

Pour half of the mac and cheese into an 8 by 8 by 2-inch baking dish. In a mixing bowl, toss the bread crumbs together with the melted butter, parsley, pancetta (optional), and salt to taste. Top the mac and cheese with the bread crumb mixture, and bake 15 minutes or until the topping has nicely browned and the pasta is bubbly and creamy (Serves 4).

My Favorite Dinner Party Recipe
Lemon-Garlic Salmon
with Rice and Vegetables

Ingredients

4 (6–8 oz) salmon filets

Lemon, cut into rounds

Olive oil, salt, pepper, and herbs

Capers

Chopped garlic

Shallots

Parsley

Onion, cut into rounds

Rice and veggies

Preheat oven to 375 degrees F.

Take the pieces of salmon and lay them on lemon rounds on a big piece of foil. Sprinkle with olive oil, salt, pepper, and any other herbs (I like thyme or any other fish savory). Add capers, chopped garlic, shallots, and parsley on top. Squeeze lemon all over it. Place big rounds of onion on top of the salmon, then place another layer of lemon rounds on top of the onion. Close up the foil tightly and put it in the oven for 20 to 25 minutes. (You can add veggies to the bag if you like.) While the salmon is cooking, you can do a quick boil or steam of green beans or broccoli and make a pot of brown or white rice. This can all be prepared beforehand so you don't have to spend too much time in the kitchen. Serve a mixed salad to start. For the main course, place the salmon, veggies, and rice out family-style. It is a nice, tasty, healthy, social dinner, but you have spent 25 to 30 minutes in the kitchen (Serves 4 or more).

Every Woman Should Own:

- A set of personalized stationery.
- An umbrella that she isn't embarrassed to be seen with.
- A great clutch/evening purse.
- A kiss-ass pair of stilettos.
- A cashmere sweater or wrap.
- Real jewelry . . . that she bought for herself.
- A great blazer.
- A quality set of pots and pans.
- A fantastic yet practical piece of luggage.
- Her style.

Here is the original, brilliant list by Pamela Redmond Satran:

A woman should have enough money within her control to move out and rent a place of her own, even if she never wants to or needs to.

A woman should have something perfect to wear if the employer or date of her dreams wants to see her in an hour.

A woman should have a youth she's content to leave behind.

A woman should have a past juicy enough that she's looking forward to retelling it in her old age.

A woman should have a set of screw drivers, a cordless drill, and a black lace bra.

A woman should have one friend who always makes her laugh . . . and one who lets her cry.

A woman should have a good piece of furniture not previously owned by anyone else in her family.

A woman should have eight matching plates, wineglasses with stems, and a recipe for a meal that will make her guests feel honored.

A woman should have a feeling of control over her destiny.

Every woman should know how to fall in love without losing herself.

Every woman should know how to quit a job, break up with a lover, and confront a friend without ruining the friendship.

Every woman should know when to try harder . . . and when to walk away.

Every woman should know that she can't change the length of her calves, the width of her hips, or the nature of her parents.

Every woman should know that her childhood may not have been perfect, but it's over.

Every woman should know what she would and wouldn't do for love or more.

Every woman should know how to live alone . . . even if she doesn't like it.

Every woman should know whom she can trust, whom she can't, and why she shouldn't take it personally.

Every woman should know where to go, be it to her best friend's kitchen table or a charming inn in the woods, when her soul needs soothing.

Every woman should know what she can and can't accomplish in a day . . . a month . . . and a year.

TAKE NOTE: Make your own "Every Woman Should" lists. Just remember when you say "every woman," you really mean *you*.

I truly believe that as women, we have more in common than we think. I take great joy in reading Pamela's list over and over again and always discovering that I want to be "that woman," too. Pamela's list inspired me to create my own "Every Woman Should" lists, and I hope your "Every Woman Should" lists will inspire other women.

Every woman should know:

_____

_____

_____

_____

_____

_____

_____

_____

_____

_____

_____

_____

_____

_____

_____

Every woman should know how to:

_____

_____

_____

_____

_____

_____

_____

_____

_____

_____

_____

_____

_____

_____

Every woman should own:

_____

_____

_____

_____

_____

_____

_____

_____

_____

_____

_____

_____

_____

_____

_____

_____

What I know for sure about . . . elegance:

You are not born with it.

It can be simple or decadent.

It is ageless.

It is underrated.

Anyone can learn it.

Everyone should learn it.

A little goes a long way.

It will never go out of style.

Mami and Papi:
A picture of good
old-fashioned
elegance.

Your Turn

What I know for sure about . . . elegance:

_____

_____

_____

_____

_____

_____

_____

_____

My parents and I in New York City.

Chapter Three
. . . .

I'll Be There for You

Navigating Relationships
with Men, Family, and Friends

"The best thing to hold on to in life is each other."
—Audrey Hepburn

ELATIONSHIPS MAKE LIFE fun, interesting, complicated . . . and worth it. The women I respect and admire most are able to navigate all of their relationships in a
way that seems effortless. Family, friends, lovers, cowork-
ers. Long-distance, online, next-door neighbors. Old and
new, casual and close. They have the balancing act down
pat, and they make it seem so easy. But as we all know, anything that *looks* easy usually takes a lot of effort.

Nothing about relationships is straightforward. Each
relationship comes with its own set of rules. You don't
treat your best friend the way you treat your mother. You
don't treat your mother the way you treat your coworker.
And you don't treat your coworker the way you treat your

boyfriend (let's hope). So, let's break this chapter down into the three main categories: men, family, and friends. From first dates to Thanksgiving dinners to girls' nights out. In each section, I have included a conversation with someone in my life whom I admire, because the best part of relationships is being able to sit down and chat with someone you adore and respect.

"And in the end, the love you take is equal to the love you make."
—Paul McCartney

My main man, Papi. [Credit: Mabel Rodriguez]

MEN

What I wish I knew about men, back then . . .

When I think back to my twenties, I would like to change quite a bit about how I handled my relationships. I was immature, and made some mistakes that I couldn't understand back then. One of the things I regret the most is not allowing myself to find a balance. One of my first serious relationships was with my high school sweetheart, who I married when I was twenty-two. When we got married, my career was just taking off and I was very excited about it all. I was so focused on my job that all I did was work and my guy took the back seat. In that relationship it

"Sometimes I wonder if men and women really suit each other. Perhaps they should live next door and just visit now and then."

—Katharine Hepburn

was all about my world, my career, my family, my friends. My world became his world. I didn't have much time for him so he found someone who did. I got divorced when I was twenty-six. Now I realize how unbalanced everything was. I wish I realized it then, or at least before I got into my next serious relationship.

My next serious relationship came almost immediately after the divorce and I made the man the center of my universe. He lived a very fabulous lifestyle and had the kind of job that took him around the world. I would drop everything to travel with him. At the time, I did not realize I was dropping everything for him. I thought I was just doing what I wanted and spending time with whom I wanted. And of course, I was, but the downside was that I was also not paying attention to anything else in my life. I wouldn't speak with my friends for months at a time or see my family much. Even some career opportunities were passed up just for a chance to spend time or travel with my guy. Although this was my choice, I didn't realize then how he never really dropped much to be with me. He didn't have to; I was always there. And yes, I was happy I could be there . . . until I wasn't so happy anymore. It's difficult to change the dynamics you've created for yourself for years. When a relationship is over, it's easy to say, "Oh, he was so controlling and jealous." (Even though when you were in love, you justified things by telling yourself and anyone who would listen, "He just wants me with him all the time" and "We're so in love, we can't be apart.") Looking back now, I can see that I helped create the mess I got myself into.

What I know about men today

You're not going to change him. The strongest relationships are always going to be with men who respect your life, appreciate your relationships and your passions from the beginning. And in turn, you do the same for him. I wouldn't want to be with a man who didn't have his own thing going on. There's nothing sexier than being with someone who allows you to be everything you are and inspires you to be better. It should never be just about that person 24/7. That never works (for more than a month or two). I always find it attractive when men have their life in control, a family they love and make time for, a career, friends, hobbies, dreams. It's sexy when someone has many interests and commitments yet somehow makes you feel as if *you* are the only thing that matters. (Even though you know you're not.) You must be comfortable, safe, secure, and independent within your relationship. It's about trust and self-esteem. It's not sexy when a man is too clingy, needy, jealous, and always available because he *has* to be with you. We shouldn't think it's going to be attractive to a man when *we* behave that way.

Now, I know that there are two sides to every story, and it takes two people to make a relationship great and two people to let a relationship fade. It is important to see what role you played in letting the relationship end. I know that I, too, have been responsible for each of my relationships ending (more so in some than others), yet I do not consider any of these relationships failures. I remember the good times and am thankful for everything I have learned from everyone who has entered my life. When you realize it is time to break up, it is a sad moment; however, it should not diminish the great relationship you had while it lasted. It just ended. Most things do.

Unforgettable Tip:
You're only great together if you can be great on your own.

Dating

Dating is like a game of chess. When you are standing over someone else's shoulder, watching them play, you can see every move they should make. But when it's you sitting at the table, you have no freaking clue.

My five dating truths

1. Chivalry is not dead. It's in a coma, because girls have become so ballsy. Guys learn much quicker than we do. The minute they realize they don't have to put effort into it, they won't. There are still men out there who do believe that a man should act like a gentleman and a woman like a lady. And there are guys who think that the girl should come up to him and offer to pay for dinner. Fair enough.

That's just not the kind of guy I want. I want a guy who is independent, who can afford to take me out if he asks me out. I want a gentleman.

2. The guy should do the courting. I am a true believer that courting is the guy's territory. Once the relationship has been set up, then you can do the inviting, not before.

3. You can be both independent and vulnerable. I want to be treated as a strong, independent person. But I also want to be swept off my feet from time to time. There is no reason a strong, independent woman can't also be vulnerable at times and allow herself to get swept away.

4. You've got to give props. If a man goes out of his way to open the door, ask you out, or pull out your chair, say thank you. If you want someone to be chivalrous, you must act like a lady and be appreciative.

5. It's better when you take it offline. Forget Facebook, Twitter, MySpace, and so on. Let him know that you're old school and you like the good old-fashioned telephone. Because there is nothing like hearing a guy's voice on the other end of the line . . . and there's also nothing like finding out about each other conversation by conversation, rather than having all of your business splashed across a Facebook page.

Unforgettable Tip:
Maintain an air of mystery.

Things you never discuss on a first date
(actually, the first three dates)

- Your exes.

- The diet you're on, the weight you need to lose, how big your ass has gotten, and so on.

- Anything you'd say to your therapist.

- Sex . . . much less do it.

- Any of your flaws.

- The fact that you don't understand or don't like the menu.

- Anything too personal.

- Marriage or having kids together.

- Medical problems.

- Celebrity gossip (shallow).

- Gossip about people he doesn't know (boring and shallow).

The Do's and Don'ts of a First Date

Don't

- Reveal too much personal information about yourself. Let's be honest, there are safety issues. For now, he's just a stranger.

- Stay too long. A first date should be between 1–3 hours. Know when it's time to say good night. Always leave him wanting more.

- Dress too revealingly.

- Ask him about his salary or how much he paid for anything.

Do

- Ask questions that will reveal his personality and true character.

- Be friendly and smile.

- Ask about his job, but don't talk about it all night.

- Change topics to find out what he likes and doesn't.

A CONVERSATION WITH
Michael Rapaport

I asked a few questions of actor and all-around cool guy Michael Rapaport. I knew he would have enlightening and entertaining answers.

What makes a woman unforgettable?
What makes a woman unforgettable is usually something small, like the way she laughs or may sing along to a song.

What makes a woman unattractive?
Any woman with any body enhancement is immediately unattractive to me. Anything plastic or injected freaks me out right away.

What should a girl never do on a first date?
Never talk about marriage on a first date—never ever ever in any context.

What about a woman's character or personality is a deal breaker? A turn-off?
Body odors are a big problem for me, and being overly judgmental of people's looks (things a person can't change specifically) are big turn-offs. Judging is human, but not mean-spirited stuff.

What do you know now that you wish you knew when you were twenty?

I wish I knew how to say, "You're right, sweetheart, you're totally right." Whether I meant it or not.

What advice will you give your sons about girls and dating?

I'll tell them to memorize this line and say it as much as they can: "You're right, sweetheart, you're totally right." And I'll tell them that just because she's "your girlfriend," it doesn't mean she's "yours." Knowing that would've helped me out a lot with women.

What's the difference between a beautiful twenty-five-year-old woman and a beautiful forty-five-year-old woman?

The difference is in the depth of the beauty. It's like a dumb, cute puppy and a fully grown, well-adjusted dog. I probably shouldn't use the puppy-dog reference when referring to women, though.

Do you think most men notice elegance, class, self-respect, and style? And is it important?

I don't know about most men, but I definitely do. Every man or woman will be attracted to someone's physical appearance, but the elegance and class of a woman is what's going to keep you attracted and coming back for more. But what the hell do I know, right? I'm paying alimony every month.

TAKE NOTE: Ask one or two of your favorite guys (a friend, a boyfriend, a husband) to answer these same questions. It's always enlightening to get the boys' perspective.

What makes a woman unforgettable?

_____

_____

_____

_____

_____

What makes a woman unattractive?

_____

_____

_____

_____

_____

What should a girl never do on a first date?

_____

_____

_____

_____

_____

_____

What about a woman's character or personality is a deal breaker? A turn-off?

_____

_____

_____

_____

_____

_____

_____

What do you know now that you wish you knew when you were twenty?

_____

_____

_____

_____

_____

What advice will you give your sons about girls and dating?

_____

_____

_____

_____

_____

What's the difference between a beautiful twenty-five-year-old woman and a beautiful forty-five-year-old woman?

_____

_____

_____

_____

_____

Do you think most men notice elegance, class, self-respect, and style? And is it important?

_____

_____

_____

_____

_____

TAKE NOTE: *Turn-on/Turn-off*

Unforgettable Tip:
....
Never settle.

I have been in great relationships and not-so-great relationships. What I have learned is that whenever I took a step back, the great relationships were always with men who had all of the qualities on my turn-on list, and the not-so-great relationships were with men who had at least one or two of the qualities on my turn-off list (sometimes all of them).

Make a list of five or six qualities you look for in a partner. And the five or six you certainly do not.

Turn-ons:	Turn-offs:

My Lists

Turn-ons:	Turn-offs:
Kindness	Self-consciousness
Humor	Insecurity
Sensitivity	Promiscuity
Strength	Neediness
Loyalty	Obsessiveness
Talent	Rudeness
Social skills	Selfishness
Easy to be around	Jealousy
Open-minded	Self-centered
	Overly flirtatious
	Control freak

Family

Family relationships can be tricky, mostly because you're stuck with the hand you're dealt, for better or worse. But they can also be incredibly beautiful, because these are the people who have known you forever, who love you unconditionally, and who are most likely going to be there for you, no matter what. These are the people who will help

My entire clan during Christmas '08. I set the self-timer.

you bury the body first and then ask you, "Why did you
do that?" Be nice to them. (I know, very *Sopranos*, but you
know what I mean.)

Families teach us about unconditional love and acceptance. They show us who we are and challenge us, because they're not going to take any of our bull. And of course, they have the ability to annoy the hell out of us. We've all got that one family member who always makes us want to stand up in the middle of Thanksgiving dinner and stab him with our fork. And yes, some of us have more than one. There are people in my family who rub me the wrong way, and I used to let it bother me a lot more. I used to be confrontational. It has taken me a while to realize that they are who they are, and you have to respect them as family members. I stay away from the topics and situations that I think are going to ignite an argument. You can choose to add fuel to the fire or add water to the fire. And sometimes, when you stop arguing and start listening and asking questions, you can find out that you have more in common than you think.

"The family—that dear octopus from whose tentacles we never quite escape, nor, in our inmost hearts, ever quite wish to."

—Dodie Smith

Family Matters

Instead of waiting until the meal is over, enjoy your time with your family. They are the only ones who can tell you about your roots. At your next family gathering, ask questions and start conversations. Do you know:

- The original town your family comes from?
- When your family immigrated? And from where?
- How your parents and grandparents met?
- What your ancestors did for a living?
- The origin and meaning of your last name?
- Your uncle's first job?
- Your aunt's favorite city?

TAKE NOTE

Come up with more questions along these lines.

_____

_____

_____

_____

_____

What makes a woman unforgettable?

_____

_____

_____

_____

_____

_____

What makes a woman unattractive?

_____

_____

_____

_____

_____

_____

If you were single today, what would you look for in a man?

_____

_____

_____

_____

_____

_____

What's the difference between being beautiful when you're twenty and being beautiful when you're fifty or sixty?

_____

_____

_____

_____

_____

_____

What was the most important thing you taught your children?

_____

_____

_____

_____

_____

_____

What is the most important thing you've learned about yourself, and how old were you?

_____

_____

_____

_____

_____

_____

What is your greatest extravagance?

_____

_____

_____

_____

_____

How do you grow old gracefully?

_____

_____

_____

_____

_____

How would you describe yourself in your teens? Twenties? Thirties? Forties? Fifties? Sixties? . . .

_____

_____

_____

_____

_____

_____

New Jersey, circa 1986. Obviously everyone had the same hairstylist . . .
ME! Sometimes less is just less!

Friends

Growing up in New Jersey, there were unspoken rules
about friendship that everyone knew but nobody talked
about. Here are some examples:

- Never ever *ever* talk about a friend behind
  her back. You got something to say, you say
  it right to her face.

- When one of you asks, "Does this make my
  butt look big?" and the answer is yes, the

"And if you threw a party, invited everyone you knew . . . You would see the biggest gift would be from me . . . And the card attached would say, Thank you for being a friend."

—*Andrew Gold*

correct response is, "Not the most flattering, why don't you try this on?" and hand over your best black dress.

- Always tell each other when you've got something in your teeth.
- My closet is your closet.
- If one of you is going to jail, both of you are going to jail.
- If one of you is going to Bon Jovi, you're both going to Bon Jovi.

There were other rules, of course, but these were some of the basics. Looking back, I realize it was the purest form of

"*Take my hand*
and we'll make it,
I swear."
—*Bon Jovi*

friendship. I learned how to be a friend and how to have a friend. It all came down to loyalty, mutual respect, unconditional acceptance, brutal honesty, and fierce love.

Close Friends

I have seen those magazine articles about "The Five Friends Every Woman Should Have." The Cheerleader, the Travel Partner, the Girl Who Just Wants to Have Fun, the Mother Hen, the Shopping Buddy, and so on. I don't buy that crap. Who wants a friend you can only go shopping with? Or only go drinking with? Not me. I think a true friend should be all of these things. These friends are few and far between, but they are the ones who are worth every second of your time. And you know you can call them for anything—at four in the morning, when you're crying, from a jail cell. And they'll come get you. I have six of them.

Friendship:
None of That Sissy Crap

My sister forwarded this to me a few months ago. It has been circulating on the Internet for a while, with no author attached to it. Whoever wrote it is a genius.

1. When you are sad—I will help you get drunk and plot revenge against the sorry bastard who made you sad.

2. When you are blue—I will try to dislodge whatever is choking you.

3. When you smile—I will know you are thinking of something that I would probably want to be involved in.

4. When you are scared—I will rag you about it every chance I get until you're not.

"It's the friends you call up at four AM that matter."
—Marlene Dietrich

5. When you are worried—I will tell you horrible stories about how much worse it could be until you quit whining.

6. When you are confused—I will try to use only little words.

7. When you are sick—stay the hell away from me until you are well again. I don't want whatever you have.

8. When you fall—I will laugh at your clumsy ass, but I'll help you up, too.

9. This is my oath, I pledge it to the end. Why?

10. Because you are my friend.

Balancing Friends

I realize I'm not the perfect friend. I travel a lot, and I struggle sometimes to balance the things in my life that I love. I don't have many super-close friends, but the ones I do have are the most understanding friends anyone could ask for. Weeks or months can pass where they don't hear from me. I'm so grateful for the friends who never give up on our friendship and always reach out to me and let me know they are there. That's why the moments we do spend together are special, and I'm 100 percent present.

But I have to admit, sometimes friends don't get their calls returned right away or their e-mails answered immediately. I'm not always available for important events like a birthday or a christening. I'm happy to say I have gotten a better handle on it in the last few years, but it is an effort to balance my work, my brand, my family, my man, my friends, my home, my health, social events, and so on. From time to time, all I want is to hide under the covers with my dogs and a pint of Häagen-Dazs. And sometimes I do. But I've learned that you can spend your time complaining about how you never have time to do anything you want and how exhausted you are, blah, blah, blah. (Ever notice how these people never actually get much done?) Or you can skip the pity party and use that energy to prioritize, organize, and plan your days, weeks, and months.

I found that actually writing things in a planner (the old-school way) works for me. No matter how busy I am, if it's on the schedule, I usually get it done. It seems funny to have to schedule in time for friendships, but as you get older and life gets crazier, sometimes it's the only way to make sure you nurture these relationships. In the past, I always meant to give a friend a call during my business trips to different cities and catch up a bit over a drink. Yet my trip would come and go, and I never found time or just forgot because I got so busy. Now, I call ahead and ask if we could set up a dinner. We agree on a time, and it goes on the schedule. Long ago, we used to spend hours hanging at

> *"It is one of the blessings of old friends that you can afford to be stupid with them."*
> —Ralph Waldo Emerson

the mall or sitting around at the diner. Now, we have to plan ahead and pencil each other in, and it is always, always, worth it.

New Friends

Why is it that as you get older, it's harder to make friends? It is for me. Long gone are the days when you could just walk up to a full lunch table and ask, "Is this seat free?" Don't get me wrong. It was difficult to make friends as a kid or a teen. But when you found someone you liked after talking for five minutes, you were friends. You'd talk on the phone later, walk to school together, and talk about boys after school. Now we overthink everything. I've met some very cool women, whether it's at the hair salon or a posh Hollywood event. We spend time chatting and laughing brilliantly when we run into each other but never make an effort to spend any time really getting to know each other. Is it me? Or them? I think both. I have said to myself, *I could totally hang with her*, or *We always have such a laugh.* Yet I don't ask for a phone number or offer mine. When we do exchange numbers and vow to stay in touch or go to dinner, we never do. I usually don't call because I think, *Oh, she probably has so many friends, she doesn't need another one*, or *I don't want to impose.* She's probably thinking the same thing, and unfortunately, a real friendship never develops. As we get older, we have to make an effort to cultivate friendships. When you run into the same person often and the two of you have great energy together, the potential for friendship should not go ignored. People cross our paths for a reason. I often think it may be the universe trying to tell us we'd benefit from each other's company. The truth is, if we don't get to know each other better, we'll never know.

Unforgettable Tip:
A true friendship doesn't have to have history; it must, however, have a future.

Men Friends

It's the old *When Harry Met Sally* debate.

I'm going to agree with Harry here. I think "men friends" are a myth. I know it is not entirely impossible to have good male friends, but let's be real here. A man will think about having sex with you. And if he doesn't, you'll most likely want to know *why* he's not thinking about having sex with you. The more comfortable you are with each other, the more likely you are to develop an attraction. In my opinion and experience, it is absurd to think that it won't. Guys and girls misread signals way too much. I am going to say that straight men and straight women can

"What I'm saying is—and this is not a come-on in any way, shape, or form—is that men and women can't be friends because the sex part always gets in the way."

—*Harry, in* When Harry Met Sally

never truly be "just friends" without some sort of sexual or romantic tension along the way. Maybe, just maybe, there are some situations where there is a great friendship and the guy doesn't think about sex. I just don't know any.

My sister Rosana (left), my partner in crime.

A CONVERSATION
with My Sister, and Best Friend, Rosana

My sister and I were not always so close. We got into some epic battles when we were younger. She thought I was bossy (I prob-ably was), and I thought she was annoying (she definitely was), but the great thing about getting older is that you get the chance to realize that sometimes the coolest people you know are the ones you know forever.

What do you know now that you wish you knew when you were twenty?

When I was in my twenties, I remember saying, "I can't wait till . . ." way too much! I can't wait till I graduate, I can't wait till I get that job, I can't wait till Friday night, I can't wait to quit my job, I can't wait to get engaged, I can't wait to get married. Well, you get the idea. I have learned to live more in the present. Life goes by in a flash, and your twenties are such a precious time of finding yourself and really enjoying life. I wish I would have enjoyed more of the moment and not rushed it all by.

What will you teach your sons about women and how to treat them?

I will teach them that no matter how confident, successful, or independent a woman is, she still needs to hear and feel that she is appreciated, respected, and loved. I will teach them that communication and honesty are the most important parts of any relationship.

What's the biggest mistake young women make today when it comes to dating and finding a man?

I think most women, for the most part, are afraid of being alone, so they settle or make themselves feel better by believing that "nobody is perfect." I agree that nobody is perfect, but I do believe that there is someone out there perfect for each and every one of us. I think dating and meeting new people is great, but when it comes to spending any significant amount of time with someone, he'd better be worth it. Life is short.

At what age were you the happiest?
Probably at five, but since I can't remember that far back, I would have to say right now, at thirty-seven.

At what age were you the most confident?
In my thirties.

What's the difference between being beautiful when you're twenty and being beautiful at thirty-five?
I think there's a lot to be said for experience. It's kind of like when you look into the eyes of a dog when she's a puppy. She's full of life, energy, and curiosity. You look into the eyes of that same dog when she's grown, and she can speak a thousand words in a single glance. I think that's beauty. (Sorry about the dog comparison.)

What makes a woman unforgettable?
This is a very difficult question for me, because I have a horrible memory, and for the most part, I forget everyone I meet within twenty-four hours. Sad but true. So, what makes a woman unforgettable for me is her energy. I usually remember people's energy. She can be drop-dead gorgeous, have the most amazing body, be dressed from head

to toe in designer clothing, but unless she had that certain "energy," chances are I'll have no recollection of her.

What makes a woman unattractive?
Envy. Selfishness. Dishonesty.

What makes a man attractive?
Self-confidence. Sense of humor. Intelligence. Sensitivity.

When do you feel the most beautiful?
When my five-year-old sons say, "Mommy, you look beautiful." Kids never lie.

What will you do to grow old gracefully?
I will wear age-appropriate clothes and get age-appropriate surgeries.

What is your greatest extravagance?
I'm pretty far from extravagant, but if I had to pick one thing, I'd say my house. It's the one thing I don't feel guilty spending money on.

What is your perfect idea of happiness?
When I go to bed at night knowing that my kids are healthy, warm, clean, have full bellies, and are safely tucked in.

Crissy and I, then and now.

A CONVERSATION WITH
My Closest High-School Friend, Crissy

Crissy is the high-school friend that every girl should have. She is fun, funny, a little crazy, and loyal like you wouldn't believe. Though we are now in our forties, when we get together, we can still act as if we are in Harrison High circa 1987.

What do you know now that you wish you knew when you were twenty?
How important it is to apply a workout to your daily routine.

What makes a woman unforgettable?
Her scent.

What makes a woman unattractive?
Too much makeup or her hair too teased and sprayed.

What are the qualities you look for in a man?
Positive attitude, self-confidence.

What are the qualities you look for in a friend?
Mutual respect and, most important, a friend who helps me see things about myself that I normally can't see and helps me be a better person.

What do you find most difficult about the media's perception of beauty today?
They retouch the model so much that women do believe they are actually seeing the real thing.

What will you teach your sons about women and how to treat them?
I have two boys, and I tell them that women are very emotional creatures and to be careful with what they say to them. I tell them to treat them with respect and to choose to be with women who make them better human beings.

What's the one piece of advice you've given your daughter that you pray she'll never forget?
Be yourself, and don't let anyone try to change anything about you. You are special.

What do you wish your mother had told you that she never did?
I wish she would have told me that she believed in me. Today, as a mother of three, I believe that they can make their dreams come true. I encourage them to be the best at

whatever they want to be. I tell them that they are in control of their future, and they can achieve anything they want, if they work hard and don't give up.

What's the biggest difference between the young women today and when you were growing up?
There is a lot more cosmetic surgery, and if you're not happy with something, you can change it if you have the money.

What's the difference between being beautiful when you're twenty and being beautiful when you're forty?
When you get older, you get smarter and wiser. You're more comfortable and confident about who you really are. When you're twenty, it's all about how you look and who you're dating. When you're forty, it's all about the woman you are and what you've achieved.

What do you hope to be like as a seventy-year-old woman?
Hopefully, a strong, healthy, independent woman who is proud of who she is and what she's achieved. I hope to have no regrets and truly amazing stories to share with my family and friends.

TAKE NOTE: Sit down with your best friend, and ask each other some of these same questions. Pop open a bottle of wine, and then compare your answers. I found this to be a great bonding moment.

What do you know now that you wish you knew when you were twenty?

_____

_____

_____

_____

_____

What will you teach your sons about women and how to treat them?

_____

_____

_____

_____

_____

_____

What's the biggest mistake young women make today
when it comes to dating and finding a man?

_____

_____

_____

_____

_____

At what age were you the happiest?

_____

_____

_____

_____

_____

_____

At what age were you the most confident?

_____

_____

_____

_____

What's the difference between being beautiful when you're twenty and being beautiful at thirty-five?

_____

_____

_____

_____

_____

_____

What makes a woman unforgettable?

_____

_____

_____

_____

_____

_____

What makes a woman unattractive?

_____

_____

_____

_____

What makes a man attractive?

_____

_____

_____

_____

_____

_____

When do you feel the most beautiful?

_____

_____

_____

_____

_____

What will you do to grow old gracefully?

_____

_____

_____

_____

_____

_____

What is your greatest extravagance?

_____

_____

_____

_____

_____

What is your perfect idea of happiness?

_____

_____

_____

_____

"Es mejor estar sola
que mal acompañada."
(It's better to be alone
than poorly accompanied.)
—Maria Fuentes, my mother

Your Relationship with Yourself

This is my mother's favorite Spanish saying. Whenever I broke up with a boyfriend, or if I was running with the wrong crowd, she would repeat, *Es mejor estar sola que mal acompañada.* There were a great many times when I rolled my eyes and walked away. Clearly, she didn't know what she was talking about; she didn't understand anything. Yet deep down, I knew she was right. And the older (and wiser) I get, the more I realize she knew exactly what she was talking about; she understood completely. Walking by yourself is much better than walking beside a jerk. Often, it is when we allow ourselves to fly solo that we truly discover who we are.

Taking time to be alone allows you to cultivate your relationship with yourself, which is truly the most important relationship of all. It dictates how you handle every other relationship. You have to love yourself before you can begin to give and receive love. And you have to respect yourself before you can begin to give and receive respect. It all comes back to who you are and whom you want to become. Then ask yourself, *Am I surrounded by people who are helping me to become that person?*

When I first moved to Los Angeles, I had a friend, also from New York, who moved here right after me. We became very close, but over time, I began to realize that things were a little lopsided. I was doing all of the giving, and she was doing all of the taking. I reminded myself of my mom's words, and out of respect for myself, I began to back away. Then, one day, she had the nerve to ask for more than I was giving. I was shocked and hurt, but in the end, I knew that it was time to break up (yes, it is OK to break up with a friend, just as we break up with a boyfriend). We reconnected years later, and I gave the friendship another try. I don't know why I was surprised and hurt when the drama was replayed as a sequel. I'm glad I gave that friendship a second chance, and I'm disappointed that I was let down a second time. I realize now that we are two very different people, and we live our lives in very different ways. Most important, I don't agree with her lack of ethics. I don't have any time for her needless drama. However, I still see her out sometimes, and I will always say hello and be polite and courteous,

but I'm not going to invite her over for margaritas anytime soon.

This is not to say that every relationship is going to be
perfect. Relationships take work, compassion, and understanding. But when you are hanging out with someone who
constantly brings you down, takes advantage of you, or
makes you feel badly about yourself, ask yourself why you
are still with that person. Wouldn't you rather find someone who brings out the best in you and, in return, you
bring out the best in them? A healthy, solid relationship
makes both of you better people.

You should get as much as you give, but remember, that
does not mean that you do something nice for someone
and expect something in return. In fact, if you are going to
do something for someone and hold it over their heads so
that they owe you, don't do it. Everything we do for someone else should be done purely out of love—especially for
our partners, families, and friends. Just beware of people
who ask for more and more. And yes, you should do for
each other what you can. Remember, balance is the key
with everything. I realize that sometimes not all relationships are on equal ground. For example, I'm more finan-
cially stable than some of my friends who are really
struggling to make ends meet. I enjoy picking up the tab,
whether it's a movie, a dinner, or a weekend getaway.
There are people who just enjoy coming along and never
invite me to anything in return because maybe they can't
afford it. But then there are people who invite me over for a

home-cooked dinner, a picnic, a long walk on the beach, or a barbecue in the backyard, or they'll come over, spend time with me and have a good conversation, and watch a cheesy movie with me. Those are the people I want in my life. There are things you can do that don't cost a lot but mean the world.

It all comes down to this: love is all that matters. In every relationship, you should get as much as you give. But remember to love and respect yourself first. And never be afraid to fly solo from time to time. It will teach you how to soar.

TAKE NOTE: *What I Know for Sure*

What I know for sure about . . . relationships:

They enhance our lives.

Some we choose, some we're stuck with.

No two are the same.

Some are toxic.

They shouldn't all feel like hard work.

Some are hard work.

They are not always balanced.

Some get us through tough times and through happy times. Some cause the tough times and the happy times.

My life would not be worthwhile without them.

Your Turn

What I know for sure about . . . relationships:

_____

_____

_____

_____

_____

_____

_____

_____

_____

_____

A shot from my second calendar, 1996. [Credit: Antoine Vergas Studio]

Chapter Four

Let's Talk About Sex, Baby

Sex Etiquette 101

"A dame that knows the ropes
isn't likely to get tied up."
—Mae West

EX IS GREAT. You should have it. Just not with
everyone. It is not "beautiful," "sophisticated," or
"classy" to give it away to everyone you think is cute or attractive. It's up to you to decide if you want sex to be an act
(or an experience). How you handle your sexuality says a lot
about who you are, your character, and your self-respect.
Sex and your sexuality are an important part of the complete package that is *you.* Like everything else, you will be
judged on how you handle this part of your life. Own it.

Someone once said that we shouldn't put so much value
on our virginity or our sexuality because it does not define
us. Well, if I don't put a value on it, who will? I don't overthink sex, but I've never given it away lightly or easily. I've
never had a one-night stand, and I've only ever slept with

men with whom I've been in a comfortable, and safe relationship.

No matter what anyone says, a woman who sleeps around is viewed, judged, and talked about very differently from a man who does the same. That's just the way it is. Don't shoot the messenger.

Like it or not, your sexual history will help define who you are, more so than other aspects of your life (such as how you dress, speak, look, etc.), because when it comes to sex, word gets around, spreads like wildfire, and sticks with you for the long haul.

Society seems to be blasé about casual sex for the most part. We've seen it all and heard it all, and we all know everyone is free to do what they want with whomever they want. However, although most people say they don't judge, we all do. I can tell you that I won't judge someone who is promiscuous, but it will tell me a lot about the person's character or self-esteem. A woman with high self-worth is not picking up a different guy at the bar every weekend. I know some otherwise very prim and proper women who are very careful in every aspect of their lives, but when it comes to sex, that caution and care go out the window. I'll never understand how the same women who have to wash their hands after they shake someone's hand or touch the escalator banister will let complete strangers into their bodies. It sounds awfully crude, I know, but it's true. I know too many women like this. I was sitting at a bar with a casual acquaintance, and she was yelling at me for eating the nuts in the bowl. They were "unsanitary," and I could "catch diseases from them." Later that night, she had a random guy's dick in her mouth. Hmmm. Who was the unsanitary one there? Unsanitary, insecure, and slutty. Not a good combo.

Insecurity is usually why a woman sleeps around. She is looking for a connection or attention, but bed-hopping never quite leaves a girl feeling fulfilled, or loved, or respected. Promiscuity says a lot about a woman's self-esteem (or lack thereof). Every man I know says he could not see himself falling in love or getting serious with someone who is "known to sleep around," though they also admit that they would never think they should be held to the same standard. Unfair? Yes. And perhaps it should not be that way, but it is. If you're looking for a serious relationship with a respectable man who will respect you back, you'd be foolish to think that you can check your reputation at the door. Nope, it comes right along with you.

When it comes to sex, I know women are as sexual as men, have sex as much as men, and enjoy it as much as men.

"Sex is a big question mark. It is something that people will talk about forever."
—Catherine Deneuve

But we are not men. And although we are equal, we are definitely not the same, nor will we be seen in the same way.

With that said, once you do find someone you trust, know, and feel comfortable with, you should let go of your inhibitions and your insecurities and truly enjoy yourself. Once you decide to give yourself to someone, you should really let go.

I asked my friends to send me topics and questions that should be addressed in a book about being an unforgettable woman. Well, I guess I shouldn't have been surprised when half of their questions had to do with sex. I do realize that to be a truly unforgettable woman in today's world, a girl must know how to own her sexuality. So, let's talk about sex.

My Friends' Questions

I have decided that the best way to approach this topic is to make it a conversation, so I picked out some of my friends' best questions (they sure sent me enough of them, and they have no shame) and have answered them as honestly and straightforwardly as possible. This way, I don't have to take the blame (or credit) for some of the shit they thought up. Also, I should mention that these are friends from all walks of life: Jersey and Hollywood, married and single, gay and straight, promiscuous and prude. While the questions came from a vast range of characters, my answers pretty much apply across the board.

How do you get a guy to leave after a one-night stand?

Oh, come on! Have we learned nothing from men? Just cut to the chase, and don't sugarcoat it. Say something like, "Hate to cut this party short, but I've got a lot to do today. Thanks. 'Bye." If it truly was a one-night stand, you don't want to send out mixed signals by saying, "I'll call you later," or "We should do this again." Be kind, polite, and *honest* with the other person.

I never feel guilty after one-night stands, but I do feel guilty about not feeling guilty. What's up with that? (I think twelve years of Catholic school screwed me up.)

No, I think it's your subconscious. Let's be really honest here. There is probably a part of you that is not exactly OK with one-night stands. Yes, we all know you have every

"There is nothing safe about sex. There never will be."

—Norman Mailer

right to do what you want, when you want, with whom you want. That doesn't mean you have to or that you should. That is really what this book is all about. Just because you have been behaving a certain way doesn't mean you have to continue. If there is something about your life that's not making you 100 percent happy, change it. Be *honest* with yourself.

Does anyone have sex the way they do in the movies?

Let's get one thing straight: nobody does *anything* the way they do in the movies. Honestly, I don't even think porn stars do some of the crazy moves when they're not "working." (Actually, I don't really know. Maybe they do. I've never had sex with a porn star.) The truth is, some movies inspire me. Why not let a porn movie inspire you or get you in the mood? But in the end, sex should be about whatever is happening between you and your partner at the moment.

"Sex is more exciting on the screen and between the pages than between the sheets."

—Andy Warhol

It can be as crazy or as subdued as you are both feeling. And if you feel like acting like a porn star, go right ahead. I'm sure it will be appreciated.

What do you do when you are in a situation where everyone is talking about their sex lives, how often they have sex, sharing intimate details, and so on, and you do not want to share?

First of all, you never have to discuss something just because everyone else is, especially not sex. I have been in that situation, and I simply don't disclose any intimate details. Some things should remain private. So, what do you do if somebody directly asks you a personal question (such as how often you are having sex)? Just because someone asks you a question doesn't mean you have to answer it. A truly inappropriate question deserves nothing more than a short, quick response. I would say something like "A lady does not kiss and tell," or "Well, that's just a bit too personal for mixed company." Or you can make a joke of it to avoid any awkwardness: "Fifty-two times a day, and boy, am I sore," or "Oh, we're like a married couple, we don't have sex." And then change the subject. We all have that one good friend whom we share these details with, knowing full well that the conversation will remain between the two of us.

Unforgettable Tip:
There is nothing sexier than knowing when to keep things to yourself.

But when you are in mixed company, why would you want or need to reveal your intimate information? I mean, can you picture Audrey Hepburn sitting at a dinner party and talking about how many times she goes down on her boyfriend? No! And neither should you. Simply not classy.

How often should couples have sex? (I read somewhere a few years ago that Madonna said that in a good relationship, you should have sex three times a week. That really stuck with me, especially since I learned most things I know about sex from her and her videos.)

In all honesty, there is no answer to this question. Everyone is different. What works for you may not work for me, and vice versa. I know I don't want to have sex four times a day, every day, though some people do (or so they say). And just because Sting allegedly has Tantric sex for ten hours straight (seriously?) doesn't mean the rest of us have to. How often you have sex as a couple is totally between you and your partner.

OK, this one is kind of raunchy. What does it mean when a guy keeps his eyes on the "out and in" rather than looking at you?

It just means that is what's doing it for him. If it really bothers you, say something. Or just take his face in your hands and lead him to your eyes. Or tell him how much it turns you on when he looks at you. That should be enough of a hint. Just remember, you don't want to make him self-conscious about it. Men are very visual, much more so than women. That may have something to do with it. I would not take it personally.

What do you do if your boyfriend wants to try something new, but you are just not that into it?

You should never do anything that makes you uncomfortable. There is nothing wrong with trying something new if that is what you want, but if it turns out you don't want to try it again (or even try it once), he should respect that. If it's something he *needs* to do, and you're not into it, you may have a problem. Sex is something that should be enjoyed by both of you, not just him. You don't want to engage in anything you don't like out of fear of losing him. Life is short. Do what turns you on, and don't make any apologies for it.

Does size matter?

Really, only if he's auditioning for a porn movie. Having a very small penis can affect his self-esteem, though. Some guys deal with it by buying a Porsche or a Hummer. Some guys deal with it by being confrontational, arrogant, and loud. As long as it doesn't bother him, chances are it won't bother you. However, I know some women complain of a guy being too big or too small. It's really up to you. If he's rocking your world, then who cares how big (or small) it is?

What are some good ways to initiate sex?

The same way you like to be put in the mood will probably work for him. With men, it usually doesn't take much, though. Sometimes just reaching for his hand is all he needs. Other times, as hard as it may be to believe, he just might not be in the mood. If after some sexy kisses, cuddling, and caressing, he doesn't respond, back off.

Everything in our relationship is great except the sex. What does that mean?

It is up to you. If it bothers you now, it's only going to bother you more through the years. If you are OK with OK sex, then why rock the boat? Just know that there is a difference between bad sex and just OK sex. There is nothing wrong with OK sex. Even the wildest, craziest sex doesn't seem all that after doing it for fifteen years. If the sex is *bad* but everything else is great, then it is probably worth talking about. Tell him about something you'd like to try, or initiate some new things that will work for you. If all else fails, there is always therapy. You never know if the problem is deeper than it seems. Did something happen in his past that is affecting his performance? Keep in mind that it is a sensitive subject, so be kind, loving, and understanding when talking about it.

Sex is a part of your relationship; it shouldn't be the core of your relationship. Balance and communication are key.

How soon is too soon to sleep with a guy? What is a good amount of time to wait before sleeping with a guy? Two months? Three? And how long can you reasonably expect a guy to wait? I know the answer to these questions is most likely "Depends on the situation." I don't buy that. I want numbers.

You can't possibly get to know someone in a few dates. Wait until you feel as if you know who you're with. In the beginning, everyone is on their best behavior, but as you get more comfortable with each other, the real side emerges. If there is real attraction, the more you wait, the bigger the attraction and reward will be. If it's real, it will be more intense as the days pass, but if it's just physical, that, too, will pass if the real person is not as attractive as you thought. Don't just give yourself to someone you may not even like. What's the point? If you must have numbers, let's just say that if you've been seeing someone regularly (a few times a week) for at least a month or two, and you still love everything about this guy (including how he treats you), then you'll probably go for it and not regret it. It all comes down to this: You should expect a man to wait as long as *you* want. If he doesn't want to wait, then at least you know he's only after one thing. Remember, it's not just about what he wants. Your wishes, your values, and your safety are only determined by *you*. When it comes to your body, play by your rules.

Are chocolate and oysters really aphrodisiacs? And green M&Ms?

I haven't found anything to be an aphrodisiac. It's all based on ancient beliefs and great publicity. Many studies have been done to prove that these foods increase sexual arousal, and as far as I can tell, the only conclusive evidence is that most aphrodisiacs are based on the power of suggestion rather than science. Basically, if you believe something is sexual, it probably will be for you.

There is this girl at work who always finds it necessary to tell me about her latest sexual exploits. It skeeves me out. How do I get her to stop?

Usually, people do this just for attention or a reaction. Don't give her either. Tell her straight up that you really

"Sex is a sport.
Fun, but dangerous."
—Ernest Hemingway

don't need to hear the details. If she continues, just say, "No, really. Stop." Change the topic. Excuse yourself, and walk away. After a while, she'll realize she's not getting the reaction she wants, and she will get the point.

Spit or swallow? Both gross me out—the whole damn thing grosses me out. Is it possible to avoid blow jobs altogether?

Yeah, become a lesbian. If you're not into it, you certainly won't want to do this with a stranger. So don't. I've never heard of a guy not wanting it. So, chances are, if you love your guy (and you're comfortable with him), you'll want to pleasure him from time to time. If you don't want to swallow, don't. If you just can't bring yourself to do it at all, *don't*. Some women enjoy it, but as with everything to do with sex, what you do and don't do is totally up to you.

The new guy I'm seeing is really experienced, and I'm pretty inexperienced by comparison. We're talking "he's stopped keeping count" versus "I can count my partners on one hand." This intrigues me and freaks me out at the same time. How can I bridge the gap?

First of all, why are you even discussing this with your guy? Nobody needs to know intimate details of your life, especially a guy you just met. Some things are private. This is one of them. You should discover each other naturally and not have to live up to each other's pasts. We must learn to keep some mystery about ourselves. I have a strict don't ask, don't tell policy. I don't ask what I don't want to know. I would never want to be thinking about his past experiences when I'm in bed with him. I simply don't want or need those visuals in my head. Once you open that can of worms, it's very difficult to close. It's not healthy, and honestly, it's pretty immature.

Everyone I know is either going Brazilian or taking it all off, and both are completely unappealing to me. Whatever happened to just waxing the bikini line?

As with everything, there are trends here, too. It is important to keep things tidy and clean down there. How much you want to take off is completely up to you. I like to take a look at *Playboy* from time to time, just to see what those trends are. If it suits me, I'll try it. But if you are not going to take much off, at least trim. Men are very visual, so do pay attention to your nether region. One needs to look pretty all over.

How do you recover from having sex on a first date? (Hey, it happens.) Is it really even possible to recover? (I didn't mean to. I blame José Cuervo.)

No, it doesn't just happen. You can blame José all you want, but let's face it, unless you're unconscious (in which case, it would be rape), I'm pretty sure the only one to blame is yourself. I've had too much José as well, and I just vomited. If, instead of vomiting, I took off my pants, you can bet your ass I wouldn't be having any tequila on a first date. It's called being responsible. And smart. You are in control of your actions. OK, but if it does happen? There is no sense in trying to explain, "I never do this sort of thing," or "Oh, my God, I'm not that kind of girl." Blah-dee-freaking-blah. When he asks you out again (*if* he asks you out again), it will be difficult to know if he just wants sex or if he genuinely wants to see you. If there is a second date, you should be clear about what is going to happen. You can't blame him for assuming that he's going to get lucky. If you don't want to have sex, tell him you didn't intend for things to go as far as they did and not to expect the same thing to happen this time around. If he still wants to go out, he probably understands. And if you do make the "It's not going to happen this time around" speech, you should really stick to it (and stay away from the tequila). If you end up in bed again, then you're just letting him know that you don't mean what you say. Do you really want to begin a relationship on that note?

Is there really such thing as the Mile-High Club?

Yes, there is. I'd recommend doing it only if you're on a private jet, though. I don't really want to even slightly, accidentally touch anything in those disgusting commercial-

"I think people should be free to engage in any sexual practices they choose; they should draw the line at goats, though."

—*Elton John*

aircraft tiny bathrooms, much less rub my naked ass all over it. But hey, whatever rocks your boat.

What about if one of you wants a third party?

That's just asking for trouble. I don't even want the visual of my partner doing it with someone else, let alone witnessing it firsthand. If you're just experimenting and not exclusive with someone and this is something you want to "get out of your system," then go ahead, I'm not judging. But realize that if you are in a committed, stable relationship, and this is coming out of left field, it may cause trust issues. Personally, I would never open that door. It's just not classy. Sex is best when there is trust, respect, and intimacy, an understanding between two people (unless you're starring in a porn movie). Plus, if I'm really honest (principles aside), it's like when you go to an amusement park with two friends. Someone rides alone, and it's not going to be me.

Should you ever fake an orgasm?

Faking an orgasm is like giving your dog a treat when he poops on the carpet. Your guy needs to know what works and what doesn't. The only way he can find that out is by your reaction. If you act as though you are loving something that really doesn't work for you, he's just going to keep doing it. Why would you want that? This just comes from our insecure, desperate need to please. When it comes to *your* orgasm, remember that he's trying to please *you*, not the other way around. If you're not doing something right to rock his world, he's going to let you know. You should do the same.

"*Remember, sex is like a Chinese dinner. It ain't over 'til you both get your cookie.*"
—*Alec Baldwin*

A CONVERSATION
with Jenny McCarthy

Since our early days working together at MTV, I've always been impressed by how Jenny handles herself. She is secure, comfortable in her skin, and confident of her sexuality. What follows is a conversation with Jenny.

What makes a woman unforgettable?

An STD. Ha-ha. Just kidding. It is the charm and grace of a strong woman that makes her unforgettable.

What makes a woman unattractive?

A bad personality can take away all the physical beauty of a woman.

What do you know now that you wish you knew when you were twenty-five?

To trust my own intuition over any boyfriend's, boss's, parent's, or health authority's.

You're an actress, comedienne, author, and activist. That naturally opens you up to public scrutiny. How do you respond to rude remarks or negative comments?

I try my best not to pay attention to any of that, but there is no denying that being talked about negatively hurts, whether or not the comments are true.

In a 1996 interview, you said, "People don't come up to me and say, 'Love your butt.' They say, 'You're funny.'" Love your butt. Truth is, there are many different things about you to love. What's your secret?

There is no secret. I do yoga, take my vitamins, and eat well. I am honest and tell it how it is. With me, there is no disguise. What you see is what you get.

(A little MTV nostalgia.) What is the greatest thing you learned about men (and women) when you were hosting *Singled Out*?

The women were looking for a companion, and the men were looking to get laid. Things haven't changed, even at the age of thirty-six.

What's the biggest mistake women today (young or older) make when it comes to men and relationships?

Many women (young or older) lose themselves in relationships, and they do not have their own lives anymore. A woman has to keep her own life and her own friends and not restrict herself to her partner's life with his or her friends.

What is the best way to make someone laugh or break the ice?

Reveal an extremely embarrassing moment that happened to you in your life.

What is the one thing you've thought or will teach your son that you hope he'll always remember?

Stand up for what you believe in, and don't let anyone stop you from speaking the truth.

Does being beautiful, successful, smart, and funny make it easier to have good girlfriends or more difficult? How do you deal with a jealous woman?

It is not any easier or harder. Jealous behaviors stem from our own personal insecurities. When jealousy impacts a friendship, I try to be as sensitive as possible to the issue and always keep in mind that those types of acts are not actually against me.

One Unforgettable Woman
Elizabeth Taylor

"The problem with people who have no vices is that generally you can be pretty sure they're going to have some pretty annoying virtues."

Elizabeth Taylor has lived an incredible life. She has been lauded for her beauty, her elegance, her flair, and, of course, her sexuality. She married eight times (twice to the same man) and never apologized for her lifestyle, only explaining, "I've always admitted that I am ruled by my passions." What is so admirable about Elizabeth Taylor is that she has followed these passions, lived in the moment, and still managed to keep her dignity. Was it because she "married" the men? Maybe. There is something to be said for a woman who got proposed to eight times. I'm impressed. Maybe she did a lot of things wrong. Her list is long, but she's got the diamonds to back it up. Does that make it better? Hmm. Maybe just a little bit.

SEX IN SOCIETY

All statistics here are taken from a 2007 Durex survey.

- The average person has sex 127 times a year.
- 45 percent of men and women engage in one-night stands.
- 48 percent of women have faked an orgasm.
- 35 percent of people watch pornography with their partners.
- 33 percent have had unprotected sex without knowing the other person's sexual history.

TWO DON'TS

I won't get on a soap box about much when it comes to sex, but allow me to step up to make two general statements:

- Don't be a moron. Wear a condom.
- Don't be easy or slutty. You're ruining it for the rest of us.

SEX TRIVIA

- You burn an average of 200 calories during 30 minutes of active sex.
- The vibrator was originally used to treat female "hysteria" in the nineteenth century. The vibrator-induced orgasms helped reduce the anxiety symptoms associated with the "hysteria."
- Dolphins and humans are the only known animals that have sex for pleasure.
- According to the World Health Organization, there are about 100 million acts of sexual intercourse a day.
- Sex is a natural antihistamine. It can help combat asthma and hay fever. The release of endorphins also relieves bouts of depression and can cure a headache.

TAKE NOTE: *What I Know for Sure*

What I know for sure about . . . sex:

It's better when there's love.

It's overrated (sometimes).

It's dangerous.

Sometimes there's too much of it and sometimes not enough.

We always want to know how other people do it.

It can bring two people closer or tear them apart.

I want to be good at it.

An Unforgettable Woman . . .

Is comfortable with her sexuality, confident, and always discreet. She knows she is not like a man, and she knows what she wants. She acts like a lady, even while hanging from the chandelier in nothing but thigh-high boots and a whip. She knows how to let go and have fun in the bedroom, but that invitation into her bedroom is coveted and hard to come by-it's a super-exclusive VIP A-list invite, not a cheap club with a badly dressed doorman and a pretend list of wannabes (most of whom got in by bullshitting). An unforgettable woman doesn't want to act like a man, be treated like a man, or have sex like a man, because she knows that being a real lady is more fun . . . and so much more powerful.

Your turn

What I know for sure about . . . sex:

_____

_____

_____

_____

_____

_____

_____

_____

_____

_____

_____

_____

_____

_____

_____

_____

_____

My backyard Buddha. A gift from Thailand.

Chapter Five

· · · · · · · · · · · · · ·

Something to Believe In

Spirituality and Giving

"Open your arms to change,
but don't let go of your values."
—the Dalai Lama

HAT BETTER WAY to follow up a sex chapter than with a spirituality chapter? And then follow up the spirituality chapter with a chapter on beauty? You may think spirituality has no place sandwiched between sex and beauty. *Au contraire.* That is exactly where it belongs. It is only when we tap into our spiritual selves that we truly become sexy and beautiful.

Personally, I didn't find my spiritual side until my mid-thirties. I had been in the entertainment business for about fifteen years at that point, and though I still found it to be fun, I began to realize that I needed to find a grounding force. I started reading a lot about self-development, and I put myself on a quest to become more enlightened. For the longest time, I found being spiritual a bit conflicting and confusing. On the one hand, I always knew that external beauty fades on even the most beautiful girl. We will all get old, we will all wrinkle, we will all lose our youth. What's the point? Well, maybe it's to let us know it is what's on the inside that matters. On the other hand, I work in an industry that focuses on external beauty. The hair, the makeup, the clothes—it's all far too important.

I think that because I was always talking about fashion, beauty, music, and celebrity style, I felt a need to have something more meaningful and important in my life. Don't get me wrong, I realize that this beauty thing is a serious business (many make a great living off it), but that doesn't mean we can't be spiritual fashionistas. I consider myself a strong, spiritual, caring individual, but does that mean I don't care about a red carpet? Hell, yeah, I care! I still want to look my best, wear the right clothes, and take a great picture. There is nothing wrong with discussing beauty, clothes, hair, and getting lost in a decadent evening. But I know that none of that outside stuff defines who I am on the inside, and it should not define who anyone is on the inside. There is much more to life than decadent evenings, designer handbags, and Botox.

Disclaimer: I am not going to pretend to be a perfect, spiritual being. There's no halo around my head. I screw up from time to time, sometimes royally. There are days when I stop, take a look at myself in the mirror, and say, "Stop being so negative/bossy/bitchy." As I have grown in my spirituality, I have learned to stop myself a lot earlier;

however, I recognize that I still have a long way to go before these conversations with myself end altogether (if ever). I am much more positive and enlightened than I was when I was twenty-five but not nearly as positive and enlightened as I hope to be when I'm sixty-five.

"Dear Lord, so far today, God, I've done all right. I haven't gossiped, I haven't lost my temper, I haven't been greedy, nasty, selfish, or overindulgent. I'm really glad about that. But in a few minutes, God, I am going to get out of bed, and from then on, I am probably going to need a lot more help."

—Author unknown (and very wise)

"My religion is very simple, my religion is kindness."
—the Dalai Lama

Spirituality versus Religion

Let's get one thing clear. This chapter is not about religion; it is about spirituality and finding faith, peace, and strength within yourself, thereby creating the type of beauty that can come only from the inside. You may find this peace in a certain religion, you may find it in a combination of several religions, or you may find it completely independent of any organized faith. Above all, spirituality is a journey, and I am not here to preach to you, because I'm on this journey, too.

I was raised Catholic. I think it was a great way to grow up, and I am very respectful of the religion I was raised in and how my mother handled it. She was never controlling about religion. She wanted us to understand what being Catholic meant, and we went to church from time to time. (I refer to it as "Catholic lite.") My mother made sure that faith in God was a part of our lives. I think it is important and very helpful to be raised with a religion and a basic belief system. Then, when we get older, we can start to question it. There are people who don't question it. But there

"Many people are already aware of the difference between spirituality and religion. They realize that having a belief system—a set of thoughts that you regard as absolute truth—does not make you spiritual no matter what the nature of those beliefs is. In fact, the more you make your thoughts (beliefs) into your identity, the more you are cut off from the spiritual dimension within yourself."

—*Eckhart Tolle,* The New Earth

are people who question and doubt and want to learn about every religion. I am the inquisitive sort. I could not believe that there was only one way to the truth. I'm not sure what the truth is.

I began to read about all different religions, trying to understand what it all meant. It all really opened up for me when someone gave me the book *Many Lives, Many Masters*, by Dr. Brian Weiss, when I was in my mid-thirties. Since then, I have bought this book at least twenty times, because I am always giving it away.

After reading this book, I began to read about Hinduism, Buddhism, Kabbalah, the Muslim faith, different sects of Christianity, and Judaism. I discovered that each religion had guiding principles that I believed in and that really fit in with my belief system. I began to pull from each of these religions to form my own, personalized faith.

A CONVERSATION
with Dr. Brian Weiss

Years ago, someone handed me Dr. Weiss's book *Many Lives, Many Masters*, and I can honestly say it is what started me on my spiritual journey. It has contributed so much to how I feel about life and death. *Many Lives, Many Masters* is the true story of Dr. Weiss and his patient Catherine. The book chronicles the eighteen months of past-life therapy sessions between Dr. Weiss and Catherine. Through these sessions, we learn (along with both doctor and patient) about the concept of reincarnation, past lives, and the many tenets of Hinduism, which, as Dr. Weiss writes in his last chapter, "I thought only Hindus practiced."

Many Lives, Many Masters has truly affected how I live my life. I am honored to introduce Dr. Weiss to you and to share the following conversation.

What does spirituality mean to you?

Spirituality is the awareness and manifestation of unconditional love and compassion. A spiritual person cannot be violent, bigoted, selfish, cruel, impatient, or filled with fear, because love dissolves all those negative traits. It helps to remember that we are all souls and not just our bodies or our brains. We are immortal; we are eternal. When we remember who we really are, our true essence, we know that we are spiritual beings.

What do you think is the difference between spirituality and religion?

Spirituality includes religion, but religion does not necessarily include spirituality. Many religious people are violent, prejudiced, and mean-spirited. A spiritual person, aware of the interconnectedness of all people and of the bonds of love that we all share, has reached a higher level of religion. All religions teach the primacy of love and compassion.

You have written a book on meditation. Do you advise all of your patients to meditate? What are the greatest benefits of meditation?

I do indeed advocate meditation, because its practice helps to bring more inner peace and happiness. Meditation does not have to be complex or uncomfortable. You can meditate while sitting in a comfortable chair or even while walking. Just relax your body and your mind, slow down your breathing, and let yourself become aware or mindful of the present moment. Don't obsess about the past, which is over. Learn from it, and let it go. Don't worry about the future. Just stay in the present. If you're drinking a wonderful cup of coffee, just enjoy the coffee. Be aware of every beautiful sip. The smell, the taste . . . savor these things. If you're ruminating about the past or worrying about the future, you won't even be aware that you're drinking the coffee. You will suddenly see an empty cup, and you missed the entire experience. Meditation is mindfulness of the moment.

What has been the most enlightening moment of your career?

There have been so many, but if I had to pick one, it would be the moment I realized that Catherine, whose story is the basis of my first book, *Many Lives, Many Masters*, was actually remembering past lives and not imagining them. My world was turned upside down that day. As a professor of psychiatry and chairman of the psychiatry department, I was very analytical and left-brained. My world was incredibly expanded at that moment when I learned that we never die, because we are souls, not bodies.

What do you think makes someone unforgettable?

I think when someone stands out in a positive way from the ordinary, that person becomes unforgettable. It's not just one trait. People may be extraordinarily joyful or patient or confident or beautiful. They are reaching their potential and not just existing. They are inspired and become an inspiration to others.

What is the key to living an unforgettable, fulfilling life?

The key is to let go of fear. Fear constantly holds people back. They never reach their ultimate potential. Fear blocks inner peace and joy and happiness. Love dissolves fear. As people become more kind and compassionate, an inner shift occurs. They become happier, and with happiness comes more confidence. Fears diminish and disappear. They become more spiritual, and this leads to even more acts of kindness and compassion, leading to even more happiness and confidence. These people are never forgettable.

Can you tell when someone is not spiritual? Is there something missing?

Clearly, when you see cruelty, violence, hatred, greed, or selfishness, spirituality is lacking. When you see a person who is kind and generous, patient and loving, then you are in the presence of a spiritual person. A spiritual person is other-oriented, not self-oriented.

What's the best way for someone to start on his or her own spiritual path?

The best way is by becoming aware of your own spiritual nature. Whether you do this by reading spiritual books, by meditating or visualizing, by learning from a spiritual teacher, or in any other way, just begin somewhere. Make that commitment. Some people begin by practicing acts of charity or kindness. Acts of compassion open the heart, and opening the heart is a powerful spiritual step.

What would your advice be for a young woman who is only concerned with her looks, the latest designer handbag, and gossip (let's face it, there are many)?

My advice is not to be satisfied with these things. The world, the universe, is so much bigger. Real joy and happiness cannot be found in material things. These are inner states. Letting go of fears and other blocks to our inner peace and joy requires a spiritual understanding. Find and nurture loving relationships. Fill yourself with self-love, and let this love flow out to others. Material things are temporary. Only love lasts forever.

Can you see when someone is a new soul or an old soul? What's the difference?

Really, all souls are ageless, because we are eternal. A "new" soul means a soul relatively newer to the earth. There are many other dimensions where souls exist and learn, not just earth. An "old" soul means a soul who has incarnated many times here on the earth plane. These

"The purpose of our lives is to be happy."
—*the Dalai Lama*

souls seem to know their way around; they are more familiar with this place. But all souls, new or old, are progressing along their spiritual paths toward a state of unconditional love and infinite bliss.

A Crash Course: Buddhism, Hinduism, Kabbalah

I found that the principles of Buddhism, Hinduism, and Kabbalah interested me in particular, and I began to study them in more depth. As with any religion, these are very complex, but here is my crash course on three very complicated and intriguing faiths.

Buddhism

Buddhism began in the sixth century BC in what is now modern Nepal. It is based on the teachings of Siddhartha Gautama (the Buddha, or "Awakened One"). The fundamental belief of Buddhism is that suffering is the central condition of human beings, and it is up to us to free ourselves from our own suffering; there is no outside force that is going to do it for us. Buddhists believe that through conscious effort and awareness of our own condition, we free ourselves. There are many different types of Buddhism, but they are all based around the Four Noble Truths, which explore human suffering. Here is a very simplistic breakdown:

1. *Dukkha:* Suffering exists.

2. *Samudaya:* There is a cause for suffering in the desire to have and control things.

3. *Nirodha:* Suffering can end once an individual releases his or her need to control and lets go of any desire or craving. This is called "the final liberation of Nirvana."

4. *Magga:* In order to end suffering and achieve Nirvana, you must follow the Eightfold Path set forth by the Buddha, which involves focusing on wisdom, virtue, and meditation.

"What we are today comes from our thoughts of yesterday, and our present thoughts build our life of tomorrow. Our life is the creation of our mind."
—Buddha

Hinduism

Hinduism is thought to be the oldest religious tradition and has its roots in Iron Age India. Hinduism is formed from many diverse traditions. It is the only major religion with no single founder, and there is no one doctrine or leader. There are many different sects of Hinduism, and beliefs vary widely, but for the most part, all Hindus believe:

There is a universal deity called Brahman (but they worship other deities as well, recognizing different attributes of Brahman in them).

There is a cycle of birth, death, and rebirth, governed by Karma (the belief that everything you do comes back to you).

The soul passes through a cycle of lives, and each new incarnation depends on how we lived our previous life.

"They who give have all things; they who withhold have nothing."

—Hindu proverb

Kabbalah

Kabbalah is an aspect of Jewish mysticism that dates back centuries. Nobody knows the exact origin, but no, it did not begin with Madonna. It is a very complicated, ancient tradition, which, in very basic terms, strives to explain the relationship between the infinite, eternal creator and the finite, mortal universe that he created. Kabbalists study the mystical aspects of the Torah in an attempt to understand the nature of the universe, the nature of the human soul, and the purpose of existence. The goal, in very simplistic terms, is to become more aware of the forces within the world and the forces within one's self.

"We receive light, then we impart it. Thus we repair the world."

—The Kabbalah

Did You Know? The Five Largest Religions

Christianity	2.1 billion
Islam	1.5 billion
Hinduism	900 million
Chinese traditional religion	394 million
Buddhism	376 million
Note: Nonreligion/agnostic/atheist	1.1 billion

Estimates based on data published by *Encyclopedia Britannica* and the *World Christian Encyclopedia*.

"Jesus, I'm a Buddhist, I'm a Muslim, I'm a Christian. I'm whatever you want me to be. It all comes down to the same thing. . . . You are either in a loving place, or you are in an unloving place."

—*Jim Carrey*

Walking the Walk

Saying you are spiritual and acting spiritually on a daily basis are two different animals. We can read about what it means to be Buddhist, Hindu, Muslim, Christian, Jewish, and so on, all we like. We can be experts on the subjects, in fact, but that's not worth a damn if we are not acting on it. It all comes down to this: spirituality is about being kind and being happy and constantly trying to be a better, more loving, version of yourself. Are you striving for that each day? Then you are spiritual. I know that for me, some days are harder than others. This is why I have surrounded myself with constant reminders. I have many statues of the Buddha throughout my house so that I can constantly reflect on the beauty of the Buddhist message. I have an incredible, large Buddha statue from Thailand, and it's sitting cross-legged in my backyard reminding me how beautiful life really is. And though I am not as strong a Catholic as my mother is, I do have crosses in my house to keep me in touch with my upbringing and my faith. Recently, I have added a tattoo on my inner wrist of the *om* sign from the world's oldest religion, Hindu. It means "God," and for me it represents calm, peace, and love. I have also established a few daily mantras that bring me back to my center and remind me of who I am and who I want to be.

My Daily Intentions

1. Practice being present. If you're stuck in traffic, rather than getting on your cell or worrying about a "to do" list, look around and notice what's around you—the mountains, the pretty gardens, children playing, a gorgeous sunset. If you're in a meeting, really listen to whoever is speaking. When you are in an elevator, don't zone out and ignore everyone. If you make eye contact with someone, smile and say "Hello," "Have a nice day," or "Good night." Be present always.

2. Think positive. Every one of your thoughts is creating your energy and your reality. Remember the law of attraction. When you're thinking ugly, you *look* ugly. It's true. Whenever you catch yourself thinking a negative thought, replace it with a positive thought, until you're thinking

"Happiness is not something ready made. It comes from your own actions."

—*the Dalai Lama*

only good, positive things for you and others. You'll radiate happy, joyful, beautiful energy.

3. Be charitable. I try to practice at least one act of charity a day. Some days, it means giving a few bucks to a homeless person, helping someone at the grocery store, or letting a car pass you in traffic. Other days, it means donating money to a cause I believe in or taking part in a fundraiser for one of my favorite charity organizations. No matter how big or small your actions may seem, it is going to matter to somebody else, and it is going to make you feel good about yourself.

4. Meditate. There is a reason people all over the world have done it for centuries. If you've never tried it, it only takes a bit of practice and an open mind. Guided meditations are available for download. Find one you identify with and that fits your needs. Whether you do twenty minutes or an hour, you'll feel the benefits. Clearing your mind works wonders. Releasing tension, anxiety, and worries brings out a calm, balanced, irresistible energy that is contagious.

TAKE NOTE

Establish your own daily mantras (feel free to steal mine, but also add to them and customize them for your own life and your own spiritual journey).

_____

_____

_____

_____

_____

_____

_____

_____

Meditation 101

The roots of meditation travel back to ancient times. In fact, archaeologists found a figure of a yogi meditating in the Indus Valley civilization, which suggests that meditation has been around since the very first civilization. It has always been a key component of Eastern cultures and society. In the Western Hemisphere, it has often been regarded as some new age hippie thing, practiced by granola-eating tree huggers. Slowly but surely, it is winning over the

"Be content with what you have; rejoice in the way things are. When you realize there is nothing lacking, the whole world belongs to you."

—*Lao Tzu*

Westerners. You can even download guided meditations on iTunes now—a sure sign that the West is catching on.

What is so great about it? It slows down the aging process, it makes you more creative, it decreases your anxiety, it improves your memory, it increases your happiness, it makes you more self-aware. The list goes on and on. Search "benefits of meditation" on the Internet, and you'll see.

You don't have to be an expert or be hard-core. You can escape for a few moments. There are many different forms of meditation. Some use focus, some use visualization, and some are transcendental (going outside the mind).

Favorite Meditations I've Downloaded from iTunes

- "Guided Meditation," Kelly Howell (from the album *Healing Meditation*)

- "The Secret Meditation," Kelly Howell

- "Sleep Easy Guided Meditation," Mary and Richard Maddux

- "8-Minute Power Mediation," Music for Deep Meditation

- Any guided meditation by Deepak Chopra (my favorite is the "Heart Meditation"; with his guidance, you'll actually be able to feel your heartbeat in any part of your body, therefore bringing blood flow where you choose, great for headaches)

Charity

By focusing on my spiritual side, I have become more patient, more tolerant, and generally calmer. It has brought a certain harmony to my life that was missing, and because I am grounded in that area, I am able to enjoy the giddiness

"The mind is everything. What you think you become.
—Buddha

of this great business I am in. I can talk about fashion without feeling as if it is the end-all-be-all. Most important, I have learned how to use my celebrity for good. I see it as a privilege and have become much more involved in charities and organizations that I value and admire.

Some of My Favorite Charities

- Saint Jude's Children's Research Hospital, www.stjude.org

- ASPCA, www.aspca.org

- Smile Train, www.smiletrain.org

- The Nancy Davis Foundation for MS, www.erasems.org

- The Hollywood Foundation for Autism and Parkinson's, www.hollyrod.org

"Be the change you wish to see in the world."
—Mahatma Gandhi

One Unforgettable Woman:
Mia Farrow

"I get it now; I didn't get it then. That life is about losing and about doing it as gracefully as possible . . . and enjoying everything in between."

Mia Farrow is one of the original movie stars who was also a spiritual role model. The chick engaged in transcendental meditation and humanitarian projects and adopted a gang of children, long before transcendental meditation, humanitarian projects, and adopting gangs of children was considered cool. She famously went on spiritual retreats with famed yogi Maharishi Mahesh, the man who introduced transcendental meditation to much of the world (including the Beatles). She has always been a staunch advocate for children's rights, is a noted UNICEF goodwill ambassador, and was one of the first to bring world attention to the crisis in Darfur. And yet you can't say that she had it so easy herself. She suffered through so much (a terminally ill child who died at twenty-one, multiple divorces in the public eye, and, most famously, her last husband running off with their adoptive daughter), yet she managed to handle it all with dignity and grace. No matter what was going on her life, she never stopped being a tireless advocate and a loving mother. She was there for everyone else when she had every excuse not to be, and that is the mark of an unforgettable woman.

TAKE NOTE: *What I Know for Sure*

What I know for sure about . . . spirituality:

Faith makes me a better person.

Beauty can't exist without it.

Religion and spirituality are not the same, but you can be both religious and spiritual.

It makes me appreciate and see little miracles.

It helps me focus on the big picture.

The journey is just as important as the destination.

To each his own.

An Unforgettable Woman . . .

An unforgettable woman is spiritual because she knows beauty doesn't exist without kindness, faith, and love. A pretty woman is not necessarily spiritual, but a spiritual woman is instantly attractive.

Your turn

What I know for sure about . . . spirituality:

_____

_____

_____

_____

_____

_____

_____

_____

Taken in Malibu, 2008.

Chapter Six

. . . .

Pretty Woman

Notes on Beauty

"Nothing makes a woman more beautiful
than the belief she is beautiful."
—Sophia Loren

THERE IS A reason I have saved the beauty chapter for last. In life, beauty will always come after self-awareness, elegance, relationships, spirituality, and sexuality. It is only once you have mastered these earlier layers that the beauty is ever going to matter. But yeah, it matters. Let's not lie. Your hair, your clothes, your makeup—it is important, because the way you present yourself to the world is how you wish to be seen. It's a reflection of who you are and how you feel about yourself.

Beauty: How It All Starts

I remember being aware of beauty at age ten. I'm sure I was aware before, but that's around the age when people started saying things like, "You should be a model," "You should be in magazines." That's when I started paying attention to beauty and really wanting to look good. I stressed about the clothes (or "looks," as I called it) that I wore to school. I wanted to wear makeup and shave my legs, but my parents would not allow it. I was too young, they said.

By the time I was eleven, I was sneaking blush, mascara, and lipstick in my bag, sock, or pocket as if it was contraband. It had to be done, but I could not be found out. As soon as I got to school, I'd hit the girls' bathroom with a few other secret glam babies, and we'd make ourselves "gorgeous" by packing it all on. Sometimes we'd forget to wash it off before we left school. I'd have to run past my mom pretending to be coughing, sneezing, or dying to go to the bathroom, while covering my face with my hands, books, or my little sister and get to the bathroom ASAP to wash all the crap off.

My mom was right. I was too young. But think about it. Haven't you wanted to look your best for as long as you could remember? When I was young, it was fun. We did what we liked and what we thought looked good. And it made us happy. Somewhere along the way, it got serious. Some of my friends struggled with weight, some with self-esteem issues, and some just gave up. We started realizing that we were being judged, mostly by other girls. It all became a popularity contest. It was no longer about how cute that lip color was or the bright pink nail polish. It was about fitting in, having the right haircut (for me, it was the

Dorothy Hamill wedge followed by the *Flashdance* perm).

There comes a point when it becomes obsessive, annoying, and a bit self-destructive. Let's stop the insanity and make it fun again. Beauty at its best should be effortless and natural (or at least appear to be effortless and natural). It should not be about trying to do everything your friends are doing.

What's the point in looking like each other? You should be inspired by others' beauty and share the beauty secrets that do work. But you must find your own individual, natural beauty and let it work for you.

MY BEAUTY BIBLE: THE FIVE COMMANDMENTS

I. BALANCE

II. ACT BEAUTIFUL

III. KNOW WHEN LESS IS MORE . . .
    AND WHEN LESS IS JUST LESS

IV. BE TIMELESS, NOT TRENDY

V. AGE GRACEFULLY

There are no ugly women,

only lazy ones.
—*Helena Rubinstein*

Balance

Some women are beauty-obsessed. They revolve their lives around the newest trends and beauty crazes. Other women are antibeauty. They seem to go to extremes to let us know that they don't think it matters at all. Then there are the beautiful women, who sit right in the middle of the see-saw.

I remember a few years ago when the Northwestern University women's lacrosse team was invited to the White House. There was criticism when the group photo was released, because all the girls were wearing flip-flops. To the White House? Really? Come on! How you dress speaks volumes about you. Do you really want to be yelling, "I don't give a shit about myself, you, or where I am"? Why not put that wasted energy into making yourself present-

"Sex appeal is 50 percent what you've got and 50 percent what you think you've got."

—Sophia Loren

able, modern, hell, even gorgeous. It does make a difference. Save the flip-flops for when you are running errands, hanging out at home, or at the beach. Ditto for Uggs. I love them, too, but come on!

I will agree that high heels and full makeup to go to the grocery store is a tad ridiculous. And so is injecting your face with Botox every week. We've all seen those women, and they don't look beautiful. They just look obsessed with trying to stay beautiful.

Unforgettable Tip:
Botox and Uggs are wonderful . . . when used in moderation.

The truly beautiful stay away from the debate. They are neither anti-beauty nor beauty obsessed. Instead, they spend their time finding that balance somewhere between the two extremes.

Act Beautiful

I was on a long flight recently, and there was an attractive, stylish woman sitting near me. Halfway through the flight, I noticed that she had a few glasses of wine and was chewing the ear off the man next to her. She was being loud and rude, and the poor guy looked as if he wanted to kill himself. Isn't it interesting how easily an attractive woman can make herself unattractive with a few glasses of wine and a loud voice? Don't be that chick. Lay off the wine, keep your voice down, and don't talk too much. This isn't just advice for long flights. It goes for all situations.

Over the years, I have been on planes and at parties with many stunningly beautiful people, but the woman who knows how to *act beautiful* always leaves the biggest impression. From the moment I met Cindy Crawford, I knew she was one of those woman.

A CONVERSATION
with Cindy Crawford

Cindy Crawford is just one of those women. When she walks into the room, people notice. It is not just because she is beautiful but because she acts beautiful, too. She is elegant, sexy, and confident. In all the years I have known her, she has remained consistently graceful, gorgeous, and successful.

What makes a woman unforgettable?
I think what makes a woman unforgettable is when she is confident enough to really be herself and be comfortable in her own skin.

What makes a woman unattractive?
Insecurity and pettiness make a woman unattractive.

What do you know now that you wish you knew when you were twenty?

I wish I had known at twenty how to be good to myself—how to appreciate everything that was "right" about me instead of keeping a mental list of everything that wasn't. I think there is much more social influence to grow up faster. I'm sure every mother feels this way, but in light of the speed of information and the availability of often unedited information, I feel that my daughter is being forced to identify herself as a sexual being way before she has any idea what that means.

What is your best advice on becoming self-confident?

That's a hard one. I think if you keep saying to yourself, "I want to be self-confident," that will never work. For me, it's more about behaving in a way that I can be proud of—being a good friend, working hard, loving and caring for my family.

What is the one thing every woman can do to be more beautiful?

Smile more.

What is the difference between being beautiful when you are twenty and being beautiful when you are forty?

In so many ways, I feel more comfortable with the way I look than I did when I was twenty. I guess I have a greater appreciation of all my body has done for me and the journeys it's taken me on.

What is the best advice your mother ever gave you?
Never give advice unless asked. She also made sure I knew I was loved unconditionally. I pray that my daughter feels that same love from me and that I have the willpower to keep my mouth shut unless she asks!

Know When Less Is More . . . and When Less Is Just Less

The old saying goes, "Less is more." Less accessorizing, a little less makeup, a little less cleavage. Maybe so. But you know what? Sometimes it's just less. It's important to know the difference. I've started the lists below and left room for you to add on.

When Less Is More

- Bright colors (a pop of color is great, two or more pops of color not so much).
- Makeup (you should never look like a tranny).
- Accessories (they should compliment the outfit, *not* overpower it).
- Trendy pieces (one trend at a time).
- Cleavage (a little cleavage is lovely, a lot of cleavage is vulgar).

When Less Is Just Less

- Diamonds.

- Beauty sleep.

- Hair (on your head).

- Smiling (it's always going to make you more beautiful).

- Laughter (see above).

- Luxury (have you ever heard someone say they've had enough of it?).

- Sex (see above).

Be Timeless, Not Trendy

It is best to adapt to trends mildly and keep up with the times according to your personal style. The time to experiment is when you are young—if you want to try pink hair, do it when you're eighteen. Once you get to be thirty you should know who you are and what your style is and play within it. You can slightly change your hair color and style, but unless you have made a radical change within yourself, it doesn't make sense to make a radical change in your look. Think of Jennifer Aniston. Her basic hairstyle and color have not changed that much. She alters them slightly every few years, she plays with the trends and often creates them, but she never goes too crazy. This has helped her become timeless. The same goes for her clothes. She never looks as if she is chasing the latest fads, but, rather, she is aware of them. She remains true to her basic style and picks and chooses the trends that work within her comfort zone. She will have a version of that style when she is sixty.

There comes a point when you don't have to reinvent yourself. We are not all Madonna, and even she has toned down the crazy with the years. It speaks more about your character when you know your style and have fun within that realm. It shows that you know who you are and that you are secure with yourself.

"Don't be into trends. Don't make fashion own you, but you decide what you are, what you want to express by the way you dress and the way you live."

—Gianni Versace

Age Gracefully

Nothing is going to be better than when you are twenty-five. Trust me. Enjoy it while you have it. I remember being worried about cellulite back then. I didn't have any! I mean, if

"You can take no credit for beauty at sixteen. But if you are beautiful at sixty, it will be your soul's own doing."

—Marie Stopes

you think it's hard to lose ten pounds when you are twenty-five, try losing it when you are forty-five. It's all downhill after your thirties. I'm sorry, but someone has to tell it like it is. This is not to say that women are not beautiful at every age. It's just that we are not the same kind of beautiful. We have to learn to grow and be comfortable within our skin year by year. There is immense beauty in an older woman who is not jaded but is also at ease with the fact that she is not twenty-five. But there is nothing more ridiculous than a woman trying to hold on to those glory days of her twenties. Low-rise jeans just don't ride the same on a fifty-year-old body. And that's OK.

> *"How pleasant is the day when we give up striving to be young—or slender."*
> —William James

Beauty Through the Ages

I don't buy the whole forty is the new thirty, fifty is the new forty thing. I know I want to age gracefully. I also know that it's easier said than done. Part of aging gracefully means realizing that you're forty when you're actually forty. The whole antibirthday nonsense is kind of annoying. When did we stop enjoying birthday celebrations? Twenty-eight, thirty, thirty-eight? I remember when I was little, I'd count the days until my birthday. I knew I'd have a blast, there would be games, all of my friends and family gathered, and, best of all, presents and cake! I was around thirty when I found myself saying I didn't really care about birthdays, I didn't want to celebrate them. Why? I used to love birthdays, but all of my friends and most women I know act as if they hate them. They hate saying their age and hope the day goes unnoticed. Most women just start acting and sounding like one another. When I realized I was headed in that direction, I decided to reclaim my birthday. I also try to encourage friends to think back to when they were kids and actually start enjoying the celebration of their special day—with cake, presents, friends, and anything else they want 'cause "it's your birthday!" Take it back! I feel blessed to celebrate every birthday with friends and family; and yes, I always tell the truth when asked about my age. And you should, too. Grown women lying about their age is a bit silly; after all, you're not fooling anybody. At least, not for long. One of my friends lies so much and so convincingly about how old she is. She once got into a monumental blowout with a boyfriend because she lied to him for two years about her age. He only found out when they were on their way to a romantic holiday and he stumbled upon her passport. Not only did it ruin the trip, but he almost broke up with her, because he felt that he could not really trust her. She talked and cried her way out of that one. Although they are no longer together, he is the only person who knows how old she really is. The rest of us play a guessing game. The truth is, she looks great. But

Unforgettable Tip:
Always tell your age—
with a smile.

because of all the secrecy, we probably think she's older than she actually is.

Just because I am comfortable telling my age, doesn't mean I am comfortable with the aging process. It sucks, plain and simple. I was lucky to have my looks work for me. I don't mean to sound vain, but it was because of how I looked that I started modeling and how I actually got my first TV job (it certainly wasn't because of my knowledge of meteorology). My looks also got me a contract with Revlon, my own calendar, and countless magazine covers. I was pretty, but, more important, I was young. The combination is powerful, and it's foolish to think it's not. Studies have shown that younger attractive people are offered more opportunities and are often even better paid. As I watch myself age (gracefully), I can assure you I'm not happy about it. Everything is changing. My skin, my body, my face. Everything. And nothing about it is better. I look older and feel older, and physically it's all downhill from here.

There comes a time around forty when women begin to lose that youthful, pretty aura. Although many women remain beautiful, attractive, even sexy well into their forties, fifties, and sixties, it's just not the same. A woman starts to be deemed attractive "for her age" or beautiful "for her age." Although today forty and fifty are looking better than ever, it's silly for women to believe that forty is the new thirty. Forty is still forty.

Although I'm not comfortable with getting old, I understand it. I can't change society's perception of older women, and I can't change the fact that I, too (God willing), will become an older woman—probably sooner than I'd like to think. I realize I don't seem so inspiring right now, but it's because I've come to terms (somewhat) with my aging process. Realizing that I'll never look twenty-five or even thirty-five again has brought a certain freedom to my life. There are things I can do to look my best no matter my age, but I'll never look thirty again, so I've let that go.

OK, here's the inspiring part. If you don't obsess over staying young, getting older is easier. If you focus on being the person you are today and own everything about your life right now, you'll always make the most of who you are. Youth is something we all have to let go of at some point. It's neither good nor bad; it's just a fact. The sooner you can understand that, the sooner you can start aging gracefully. Let go of the fight, and win the battle.

Beauty Through the Ages— From Goat-Milk Baths to Botox	
400 BC	Cleopatra wears eyeliner, douses herself in jasmine, and bathes in a tub of goat milk.
1854	P. T. Barnum stages the first modern American beauty pageant, but it is shut down by public protest.
1936	Chemist Eugene Schuler invents the first sunscreen.

Beauty Through the Ages—	
	From Goat-Milk Baths to Botox
1980	Coppertone develops the first sunscreen with SPF.
1982	French surgeon Yves-Gerard Illouz performs the first liposuction.
1994	The Wonderbra hits the market. "Who cares if it's a bad hair day?"
2002	Botox is approved by the Federal Drug Administration.

"Like anyone else, there are days I feel beautiful and days I don't, and when I don't, I do something about it."

—Cheryl Tiegs

Beauty Breakdown

After many years in the beauty business, I am proud to say that I have my style and image pretty well honed. It wasn't always this way. It has taken a lot of trial and error for me to find out what works for me. Let's break it down to something we can all relate to: hair.

I've been a long-hair girl most of my life. There were a couple of times when I took a chance and chopped it all off. The first time I can think of was very early in my modeling days. My designer friend and mentor Piero Dimitri set me up with an appointment at a very hip, stylish New York salon. I was still living in Jersey, and my hair was almost down to my waist and bigger than Jon Bon Jovi's circa 1984. I was told I "needed a change," I needed to "update my look," "take it down a bit," "get a trim," and on and on. OK, I thought, how bad could it be? I was, after all, entering a whole new chapter in my life. I was now a working model in New York City (even if at the end of every day, I ran back to my safe Jersey haven). I was ready for a bit of a change. After I made myself comfortable in Pepe Le Pew's chair (I don't remember his actual name,

but he was terribly French), we had a "consultation" for three minutes wherein he basically told me I had no sense of style whatsoever. He grabbed my hair in a ponytail and chopped it off at the nape of my neck with one clean swipe of his super-fancy scissors. With my massive ponytail in one hand and his scissors in the other, he said in a heavy French accent (and by French I mean "arrogant"), "You don neeed zhis."

After I finished the world's longest gasp, I closed my mouth, stared at myself in the mirror, tried really hard not to cry, and pretended to like my new, super-edgy, shaved-in-the-back, slightly butch bob. My friends were shocked. They didn't know I had it in me—and neither did I. In Jersey, I really stood out with my new look. I liked being different, sophisticated, stylish. I was no longer "hiding" behind my hair. I even carried myself differently. I walked taller, dressed a bit more elegantly. I had never noticed how long my neck was. I actually really liked my new look—for about two weeks. Then I wanted it long again. Eventually, it grew out and stayed long for fifteen years. Then I pretty much relived the whole experience again (minus Pepe Le Pew and the butch edge). These days, I play it a bit safer. I stick with what works. I decided there was nothing wrong with liking long hair or making it a trademark of sorts. I decided that for me, when it comes to hair, less is just less. I still change my style from time to time. Sometimes I go blonder, sometimes super-layered, sometimes one length, maybe curly or straight, but always long. What can I say, I'm a long-hair girl.

When you're young, it's cool to change your look and

experience a bit with your image, but as you get older, you should have your look down. You still need to check the trends as you would when it comes to clothes. Hair trends change with the seasons. It's important to choose cuts and styles that fit your image. For example, if you're a long-hair girl, check out what's going on with highlights. Are they chunky, blended, obvious, beachy, or sophisticated? Do you need highlights or lowlights? Is one length in, or are choppy layers all the rage? Bangs are always making a comeback, but sometimes they're sharp and heavy, others light and blended. Cutting bangs is a great way to change your look without a long-term commitment, since they grow out in a few months. If you're a short-hair girl, you can get a modern pixie, layer it into a sexy shag, or grow it a bit for a sophisticated bob. Being aware of hair trends will help keep you looking modern, fresh, and current. You don't have to follow every trend or agree with what every Frenchman tells you is *au courant.* The same goes for makeup, clothes, shoes, the latest exercise craze. Decide what works for you, and forget the fads.

A Beauty Toolbox

After many years of working in this industry, I have gathered a few timeless tips that will ride every trend. I have broken things down here into tip boxes for each category.

Makeup Tips

Cosmetics don't last forever. Check dates, and throw out old products. They don't apply well. Mascaras dry out quickly and don't work. Liquid makeup and nail polish separate once they're old. Powders go on blotchy.

Keep your brushes clean.

Beware of cheap tools. Cheap brushes and combs, hot irons, and blow dryers will only damage hair. Good tools are worth the investment. Inexpensive or affordable are not the same as "cheap."

Shimmery eyeshadows will only highlight lines (if you are older than forty) and should be avoided everywhere but the inner corners of the eye.

Go to a makeup counter for lessons and samples. They will also be able to help you determine your best colors depending on your skin, eye, and hair color. (This is also great to do if you are going to a party—you'll get your makeup done for free!)

Makeup Tips

Don't forget the rest of your skin. You don't have to apply makeup all over your body, but your powder or foundation should go at least to neck or décolletage, depending on what you're wearing.

If your arms and legs are showing, make sure you moisturize, and dust a bit of glow on with some bronzer so you look even all over.

The older you are, the less makeup you should wear. Once it settles into lines, you just look older. Tinted moisturizers work better than heavy bases or powders on more mature skin.

"The most beautiful makeup of a woman is passion. But cosmetics are easier to buy."
—Yves Saint Laurent

Applying my own lashes behind the scenes at a shoot for my Kohl's line.

Hair Tips

When you're having a bad hair day, a simple tousled updo or neat bun always looks sophisticated and elegant and works for day or night.

Don't overexpose your hair to the sun. Nourishment and protection are key when facing the elements. If you are going to be in the sun for an extended period of time, use a UV filter product and a hat.

Look for products that are paraben- and sulfate-free. (Parabens are synthetic preservatives that have been proven to be unsafe. Sulfates are harsh cleansers that strip the hair of its natural moisture and shine.)

When choosing a hair color, the natural shades and colors (think of the color a child would have) will help you look younger and more modern. Bright reds, oranges, and funky tones may be fun on an eighteen-year-old but will only age anyone older than thirty-five.

Deep-condition your hair once a week.

Update your hairstyle at least every two years.

Life is an endless struggle full of frustrations and challenges, but eventually you find a hair stylist you like.

—Author unknown

Body Tips

I certainly take better care of my body now than when I was in my twenties. I have to, if I want it to look its best, because I know that if I don't feel good, I don't look good. I do this by eating mostly vegetables, fruits, and lean meats (mostly chicken and fish). I snack on fruit, veggies, nuts, and some cheese. My favorite dip is hummus, and I like to make it myself so I am sure that it is fresh and healthy. I used to eat a lot more junk food. By chang-

[Credit: Daniela Federici/D.R. Photo Mgmt.]

ing my eating habits, I have improved my overall appearance, from my body to my skin to my hair. It wasn't easy, as I've been a junk-food junkie most of my life. But I tried and tried again, and now I manage to eat healthy, natural, unprocessed foods most of the time. I really do feel better for it. That doesn't mean I don't enjoy the occasional pizza, burger, or beer whenever I desire. It's just that these days, I desire that sort of stuff a lot less. If you truly want to look good at any age, you must have discipline and patience, and you must commit to taking care of yourself inside and out.

My Top Body Tips

Getting into the right mind-set is key. Work out every day for at least thirty minutes. With each workout, remind yourself that you are getting leaner, stronger, and healthier (even if you don't always feel it).

Find a routine that works for you and that you won't dread doing every day. There are tons of options: hiking, dancing, Pilates, yoga, running, ballet, biking, swimming, walking. Whatever it is, just move! I have found that Pilates works best for me, and I endorse Mari Winsor's Pilates DVDs. I've launched Daisy Fuentes Pilates for the Wii, which is great because it's interactive fun and you can do it at home.

My Top Body Tips

Find out what motivates you. For example, I remind myself how bad I feel when I've eaten too much. I hate this uncomfortable feeling, so I am always aware of allowing myself to be satisfied instead of full. I also remind myself of how much better I'll look in my clothes if I am a few pounds lighter. I love fashion, so this is a great motivation for me! Find a tool that works for you. Go toward your goal, and be proud of everything you do to improve your life and your health.

Stretch! As I make my coffee and toast in the morning, I do all of my stretching. I use the counter as a ballet bar. I try to stretch a bit more each day.

Try to make healthy, light food choices as much as possible.

Avoid dips. I love dips and snacks, but it is much healthier when I make my own. I like a fresh salsa with tomatoes, onions, garlic, olive oil, jalapeño peppers. You can also dip carrot or celery sticks in homemade hummus.

Keep grapes and cherries and raw nuts on hand for picking and snacking.

My Top Body Tips

I find that a low-fat, low-carb diet works best. Low-carb means good carbs: bran, brown rice, oatmeal, whole grains, and so on.

There are so many crazy diets out there, but I believe that you don't have to cut out any one food group. It's all about small portions of lean meats, whole grains, and plenty of fruit and veggies.

Some things you should definitely cut out:
    Cigarettes
    Fried foods
    Sodas
    Saturated fats
    Sugary snacks
    Store-bought chips
    Full-fat cheeses
    Doughnuts
    Too much alcohol

Remember that a good, healthy, balanced diet is essential to make your workouts effective.

Drink water!

"If I listened to my body, I'd live on toffee pops and port wine. Don't tell me to listen to my body. It's trying to turn me into a blob!"
—Roger Robinson, New Zealand's master runner

Skin Tips

Suncreen! I did most of my sun damage in my late teens and early twenties. In my defense, we didn't know as much about UVA and UVB rays back then, and we didn't have proper sunblock. Today there is no excuse.

Avoid too much sun exposure, and wear SPF always. Don't overdo it with the faux tanning lotions and sprays. Orange skin is never in and never chic. Nothing will date you more than orange or overburned skin. A nice sun glow looks wonderful, but "I went on vacation and fried myself" looks stupid.

Use at least SPF 30 on your face every day. I like Neutrogena Ultrasheer SPF 30. Olay tinted moisturizer is also good for most skin shades.

Use at least SPF 15 or 20 on your body. You will still get tan!

Grooming Tips

Wax or laser any facial hair (don't forget the magnifying mirror).

Wax or laser any hair on hands and knuckles.

Wax or laser any hair on feet and toes.

Wax or laser bikini area (if you don't take it all off, keep what's left trimmed short and neat).

Wax, laser, or shave legs and underarms.

Hair on arms is fine if it's not too thick or too dark. If it's too dark, you can lighten it with facial bleach available at a drugstore. If it's dark and thick, wax or laser. Don't shave.

Whatever you decide to shave, do it at least every other day.

Style Tips

Select styles that work with the shape you are in right now—not the shape you were in five years ago or the shape you're going to be in a "few months." Fit is everything.

Find the colors and cuts that work for you, and stick to them, no matter what the season's trends say. If orange is in but orange looks horrible on you, forget it! If miniskirts are all the rage but your legs aren't in great shape, don't bother!

Take note of what you are wearing when you get the most compliments. I am complimented when I wear fuchsia or red, so I know they are good colors for me.

Don't always stick to black just because it's safe. Be bold, and try colors and patterns, but do it in moderation. You don't want the clothes to be so loud and busy that they detract from your face.

There is something to be said for common sense here. There is never going to be a definitive chart of what works for your body and your coloring. There are no set rules. Trial and error is the way to go.

If you are not comfortable in it, it's never going to look good.

[Credit: SPICER/spice-photo.com]

"A girl
should be two things:
classy and fabulous."
—Coco Chanel

Martyn and I.

A CONVERSATION
with Martyn Lawrence Bullard

Martyn is one of the most fabulous people I know. He is so English, the guy to call when you have a question about chic people, places, or things. He is an interior decorator to some of Hollywood's wealthiest and most famous, so he knows a thing or two about glamour and beauty.

What is the most beautiful aspect of a woman?

Good old-fashioned grace. The elegance of a restrained gesture, just the slightest aroma of perfume as she passes by (a beautiful, confident woman never needs to douse herself in overpowering fragrances), to watch her take her seat keeping her legs demurely close, just revealing enough calf to send a man wild. The bat of an eyelid, done with great confidence, yet still knowingly shy and enticing. The old-fashioned elegance of waiting for a man to open a door and letting her walk in first or closing her into a car as she seductively pulls in her stockinged leg. The grace and understanding of these attentions is so seductive. Yes, to me there is nothing sexier than a graceful woman who knows how to behave . . . and when not to!

What is the best beauty advice you can give a woman?

One of the most important pieces of advice I can give is stolen from the great George Benson/Whitney Houston song "The Greatest Love of All." Just listen to the lyrics and soak up that advice, because, as it says, learning to love yourself *is* the greatest love of all. Show yourself and others all the beauty you posses inside, and by learning to love yourself, embracing all your faults, whatever they may be, and seeing those faults are really just a part of us and by accepting this love them, yourself, and eventually everyone will love you, and through that inner love your outer beauty will shine tenfold.

What is the easiest way to enhance your beauty?

Smile. It's that easy. Just smile. You'll be amazed. The world will smile back at you, and your beauty will have reached out and kissed so many by this simple action. A smile will take years off you, and when someone smiles, you don't think, *Oh, look how old and unattractive they are.* No. You smile back. Suddenly, beauty and happiness are instantly shared and enjoyed! And of course, age is the real pearl of wisdom and the key to beauty. As we grow older, most people think their looks are fading away and struggle with extreme methods to maintain a youthful appearance, be it fancy serums or surgical procedures, designer clothing or grueling workout regimes. The reality is that if you use all the wisdom and learnings that we gather as we grow older from our day-to-day experiences that shape our lives and take this wisdom and use it to better yourself, you become confident from all those lessons, take the good from every situation, and put that knowledge to better use in your life. Never regret, only learn from the past, and look to the future with all the knowledge you have gathered (which is priceless). Once you achieve this, you will have eternal beauty and a radiance that will exude from you. Men will be falling at your feet, irrelevant of your age!

Beauty and Style Questions

Over the years, friends and fans have turned to me for beauty and style advice. I have picked out the top five questions that always seem to come up and answered them below.

How do I follow the trends without looking like a fashion victim?

Hemlines rise and fall, heels are in today, out tomorrow, brunette is the new blond, blond is back. This is why it is important to know who you are and what works for you. Once you know this, you can work with the ever-changing fashions. There are certain trends that everyone can ride (chunky jewelry, black nail polish, and so on), but then you've got to know when to sit it out (miniskirts when you're fifty, thick belts if you have a thick waist, skinny jeans if you're not skinny). A fashion victim follows every new craze. A fashionista chooses the trends that work for her and keeps it within her established personal style.

How can I always look good in a photo?

Most people fall into a routine when a camera is pointed at them. A pout, a half-smile, a turn of the head, or, most obnoxious of all, throwing a hand or a bag in front of the face. When you take many pictures and are forced to look at yourself so many times, you learn what works and what

How to always take a good photo? No fussing, just smile.
I didn't really want my picture taken here. I just got out of the water, no makeup,
wet hair, in my bikini. I wanted to freak out, instead I just smiled.

doesn't. Here is what I have learned from having my picture taken (a lot) over the last twenty years.

Don't be shy. The whole "Oh, please, no photos," or "I'm so not photogenic," or "No, my hair's a mess" routine is just annoying. And by the way, it will almost guarantee a bad picture. Stop whining. When a camera is pointed at you, just straighten up a bit and smile. It's that simple. Really.

Keep it natural and simple. Don't lean into whoever is next to you. It's not natural, and it will just make you look crooked or give you a double chin (or both). Carry on with whatever you were doing. Natural shots are best. You don't always have to throw your arm over someone, pose, and smile.

"*All right Mr. DeMille,*
I'm ready for my closeup."
—Sunset Boulevard

Wear photogenic clothes. If you are going to an event where you know there will be pictures, dress appropriately. These pictures will be around for a while and will most likely be shown to many, so don't wear anything too trendy that will look outdated next year or next season. Don't wear loud patterns; it's just distracting. Solid colors will always look more elegant. Keep it within your style, and don't wear something a bit crazy just because it's a party. You'll just look as if you are trying too hard. Elegance, glamour, style, and comfort are key. (This all holds true if you want to look good in a photo or if you just want to look good, period.)

What's with all the new dress-code labels?

I think everyone is too concerned with labeling dress codes, as if it weren't confusing enough already. How do you define "business casual," "smart casual," "California casual," "dressy casual"? And what is the difference between "formal," "black tie," and "black tie optional"? And what the hell is "festive"? Let's try to break it down.

- Black tie: Tux for men, gown/long dress or elegant cocktail-length for women. You'd look silly and disrespectful wearing jeans.

- Formal: Elegant dress, long or cocktail-length. A dressy chic pantsuit will also work.

- Cocktail: A less formal cocktail-length or short dress. You can also do dressy trousers.

- Business or Business Casual: More conservative. Think a tailored dress, a pencil skirt, or a pantsuit. But it doesn't have to be boring! Add a few great accessories to stay stylish and not stuffy.

- Black tie optional: This just means that some men may be wearing tuxedos, and women will be in cocktail or long dresses. Don't go too casual. At the very least, a suit for the man and a cocktail dress for the woman are usually appropriate.

- Dressy casual: This is an oxymoron, and the host asking for it is just a moron. That being said, if you do come across this, you can probably get away with "informal" (a simple, stylish dress or pairing your jeans with some great heels, fabulous jewelry, or a dressier top).

- Festive: This one is the most confusing of all. What are you supposed to do, bring a disco ball? Unless you're going to a wake, every event you get an invitation for should be festive! But I'd say that this is where you pull out anything with bright colors or a bit of sparkle to it. If an invite says "Festive," it probably means there will be music, so look fabulous, and wear your dancing shoes.

When you can't figure out the dress code, is it better to be overdressed or underdressed?

Neither. You should always look well dressed. As a general rule, always go chic, elegant, and put together. Great hair, nice makeup, and a classy mani/pedi (red or sheer pink) will go a long way and make it difficult to look too shabby. When in doubt, pull out that great-fitting, modern, classic black dress and an amazing pair of pumps (a must-have for every woman). Dress it up with bold or fancy jewelry, or keep it simple with more casual accessories.

Even when I'm doing casual, I try to finish my look with an elegant, stylish coat or wrap, a fabulous bag or clutch, and a sexy fragrance.

If you're trying to dress up jeans (dinner party, festive, drink meeting) always do a dark, elegant wash. Add a dressy blouse, elegant halter, or tailored blazer. Add classy, elegant accessories, And killer high heels or to-die-for boots.

How do you plan to grow old gracefully?

I'm pretty sure I'll never get a facelift. I plan to stay on top of the latest treatments, creams, lotions, and even magic potions if they're said to work. I'll try anything that isn't extreme and has been tested and approved. I plan to delay or slow down the aging process as best I can, but I refuse to drive myself crazy doing it. It's all about moderation and balance and realizing that I have to be a bit more vigilant than I was in my youth.

Finding balance in my backyard.

One Unforgettable Woman
Audrey Hepburn

"Success is reaching an important birthday and finding out you're exactly the same."

Audrey Hepburn is often regarded as one of the most beautiful women in the world because she understood the true essence of what it meant to be beautiful. She showed women how a simple pair of black pants, a black turtleneck, and some ballet flats could be utterly fabulous, provided the woman wearing them carried on with grace and confidence. She taught the world the true spirit of charity, working tirelessly for UNICEF and devoting the final years of her life to the organization. On the Christmas Eve before she passed away, she read a favorite poem to her grandchildren, "Time Tested Beauty Tips" by Sam Levenson:

For attractive lips,
speak words of kindness.

For lovely eyes,
seek out the good in people.

For a slim figure,
share your food with the hungry.

For beautiful hair,
let a child run his fingers through it once a day.

For poise,
walk with the knowledge you'll never walk
  alone . . .

People, even more than things,
have to be restored, renewed, revived,
  reclaimed and redeemed and redeemed . . .

Never throw out anybody. Remember, if you ever
  need a helping hand, you'll find one at the end
  of your arm.

As you grow older you will discover that you have
  two hands.
One for helping yourself, the other for helping
  others.

IF BARBIE WAS A REAL WOMAN

- She would stand seven feet two inches tall and have a neck twice the size of the average human.

- Her measurements would be 39-23-33.

- She would have to walk on all fours in order to move.

BEAUTY TIPS
FROM AROUND THE WORLD

From Greece	Do your body peeling at the beach. Smear oil over your body, and massage it lightly with sand.
From England	Save your used tea bags. Keep them in the fridge, and when your eyes are puffy or irritated, lie down with the cold tea bags on your eyes for a few minutes.
From Italy	Keep olive oil in your bathroom. Use it on your hair and eyelashes for nourishment, moisture, and shine. Apply it to your cuticles and nails to keep them from drying.

From Latin America	Deep-condition with avocado. Cut the avocado in half, and rub the soft part on your hair. Let it sit for one hour, then rinse with shampoo and conditioner.
From Holland	Get fresh air. Dutch women take long strolls and bike rides to help improve their skin and overall health.
From Japan	Eat seaweed and soy. In Japan, women eat these foods to keep their skin healthy.

Beauty Items Every Woman Should Have

In Her Bathroom

- Face moisturizer with SPF (at least 15; if you're in a sunny warm climate, use at least 30).
- Body moisturizer (hydrating and firming).
- Deep conditioner, to be used once a week.
- A blow-dryer, a round brush, hairspray, and finishing spray . . . it's all about the hair.

- A magnifying mirror.
- Eyeliner, eyeshadow, foundation, and the right makeup brushes (it's best if all have been tried and tested at the makeup counter).
- Nail polish in pale pink or sheer white, classic red, base, shiny top coat.

In Her Shower

- Pumice stone or large emery board to keep feet smooth.
- Body Scrub (once a week).
- Razor—if you feel stubble, use it.

In Her Purse

- A nail file.
- A hand mirror.
- Perfume.
- Lip gloss.
- Breath mints.
- A couple of safety pins.
- Band-Aids (in case shoes hurt or cut your feet).

In Her Closet

- A little black dress or three.
- A great pair of black stiletto pumps.
- A perfectly tailored pant suit that can be worn as separates as well.
- Dark wash jeans that fit perfectly.
- A cashmere sweater.
- A crisp white shirt.
- A trench coat.
- A cocktail ring.
- A good watch.
- An expensive piece of jewelry . . . that she bought herself.
- Black high-heel boots.
- A full-length mirror.
- Good lighting.

TAKE NOTE: *What I Know for Sure*

What I know for sure about . . . beauty:

   It truly is in the eye of the beholder.

   It can be found in the most unexpected ways.

   It can be cultivated and perfected, but it can also be stumped and tarnished.

   Some people and some things only get more beautiful with time.

   External beauty fades; internal beauty is for-ever.

   It's important.

   Everyone has it, but not everyone knows how to use it.

   It's always around us, and it should not be taken for granted.

Your turn

What I know for sure about . . . beauty:

_____

_____

_____

_____

_____

_____

_____

_____

_____

_____

_____

_____

_____

_____

DAISY FUENTES

HEIGHT 5'10" • HAIR Brown • EYES Brown • SHOES 9 • 35B - 25 - 35 • SIZE 6-8
HAUTEUR 1.78 • CHEVEUX Bruns • YEUX Bruns • CHAUSSURES 40 • 89 - 64 - 89 • TAILLE 36-38
SAG • AFTRA

Special Bookings

My first official modeling card for IMG. Photo taken circa 1989 in New York.

My Back Pages

Letters and Questionnaires

"Ah, but I was so much older then,
I'm younger than that now."
—Bob Dylan

A Letter to My Twenty-Year-Old Self (Dedicated to Women of Every Age)

Dear Daisy,

Slow down. Look around. It's not going to be like this forever. Enjoy it. The good and the not so good.

I know you think you know everything right now. I know you think you have it all figured out. But darling, you don't know the half of it. You are going to grow in ways that you cannot imagine. You have more potential than you realize. Give yourself more credit, and take more chances. Don't take any crap from anyone. Believe anything is possible. Dream big. Life has major plans for you even if you don't. Open your life to the unfamiliar, even when it's frightening. Especially when it's frightening. Especially when it's frightening. Discover the world around you. It is going to shock you, surprise you, delight you, scare you, awaken you, and shape you.

You are going to realize that no matter how much you learn and no matter how much you experience, there will always be miles to go . . . and that is a fabulous thing. There will always be room for improvement. You can choose to look at this as a daunting task or an incredible journey. Choose the incredible journey.

Everything really does happen for a rea-

son. Except watching someone you love be ill
or die. I don't think you'll ever quite understand that one. I'm not sure you're supposed
to. But you do have to accept a certain
fate.

Have fun. Have more fun than you think
you deserve. Laugh loud, take chances,
spend hours sitting by the pool, read the
gossip rags, sleep late, treat yourself
often . . . and don't apologize for any of it.
But don't forget to enrich your soul, search
for enlightenment, be kind, compassionate,
and courteous. Smile at strangers, donate
money to charity, hold doors for others, say
thank you when people hold doors for you.
Talk to the woman at the party whom you
have the least in common with; it is going to
open your life up in ways you cannot imagine. Everyone who enters your life does so
for a reason.

Give up the need to know why things

happen the way they do. Don't overanalyze everything and everyone. It is a waste of your precious energy. Understand that there are things you cannot change, but by embracing them you will find happiness.

Refrain from being judgmental or jealous. And never blame others for what happens or does not happen to you. You, and only you, are in control of your actions and reactions. You choose how you respond to crisis, turmoil, love, and happiness. Make positive changes in your mind, and your life will follow. Lighten up; don't be such a hard-ass. Don't be so hard on yourself or others, especially those who love you.

Forgiveness is an act of consciousness; it will liberate your spirit. So forgive those who have hurt you. Realize that you hurt others too, even if you don't mean to. And when you are self-destructive, negative, rude, disrespectful, angry, or resentful, acknowledge it and forgive yourself. Start again, because it is never too late to be the person you imagine yourself to be. And never, ever stop striving to be that person.

Dare to live an unforgettable life, and whatever you do, be anything but ordinary.

And remember, in the end, the only thing that truly matters is love.

I wish you love. May you always be blessed, graceful, and thankful.

Love,

Daisy

Final Words

It is a combination of many qualities and traits that makes someone unforgettable. Some do have to work harder at it than others. The process of improving yourself and becoming a better, more beautiful you does not end at a certain age. I believe that is why some only get more beautiful with time. You have all you need within you.

I really do hope this book helps you to achieve goddess-like beauty and enhances who you are, even just a little bit. Remember that there is always room for improvement. When you're trying to become a better person, everything counts. We are living in a world where how you look matters, but don't forget that it's how you behave that speaks volumes about who you really are. It does not matter how beautiful you are if you behave ugly. Find your composure, and keep it, even when you temporarily lose it. Don't let your ego get the best of you, or even the worst of you. Find a way to lose your ego every time you see it. Act from your heart. Your light really does shine from the inside out. Yes, you will be judged on your appearance, so go ahead and have a fantastic time making yourself gorgeous. Learn new makeup tricks, read the fashion mags, lose a few pounds, wear the latest trend or be incredibly classic, but be fabulous. Just don't get caught up in superficiality. Expand your mind, read, ask questions, learn what you don't know, even what you don't really care to know. And no matter how much you learn, don't be a know-it-all. Only a fool knows everything.

I understand that in today's society, everyone has strong opinions and beliefs. So do I. I try not to judge others, so don't judge me. This is my take on life and beauty.

Dare to be unforgettable,

Daisy

My Proust Questionnaire

As I mentioned at the beginning of this book, *Vanity Fair* ends each issue with the Proust Questionnaire, which they have a featured celebrity fill out. I think it's a great way to end this book, because a truly unforgettable women never stops asking questions (of herself and of others). I have included several blank Proust Questionnaires. Answer the first one yourself (go ahead, fill out the Proust one again, and see if your answers have changed at all). Have some of your favorite people fill out the others.

Proust Questionnaire by

_____

1. What is your idea of perfect happiness?

2. What is your greatest fear?

3. What is the trait you most deplore in yourself?

_____

_____

4. What is the trait you most deplore in others?

_____

_____

_____

_____

_____

5. Which living person do you most admire?

_____

_____

_____

_____

_____

6. What is your greatest extravagance?

_____

_____

_____

_____

_____

7. What is your current state of mind?

_____

_____

_____

_____

8. What do you consider the most overrated virtue?

_____

_____

_____

_____

9. On what occasion do you lie?

_____
_____
_____
_____
_____

10. What do you most dislike about your appearance?

_____
_____
_____
_____
_____

11. Which living person do you most despise?

_____
_____
_____
_____
_____

12. What is the quality you most like in a man?

_____

_____

_____

_____

_____

13. What is the quality you most like in a woman?

_____

_____

_____

_____

_____

14. Which words or phrases do you most overuse?

_____

_____

_____

_____

_____

15. What or who is the greatest love of your life?

_____

_____

_____

_____

_____

16. When and where were you happiest?

_____

_____

_____

_____

_____

17. Which talent would you most like to have?

_____

_____

_____

_____

_____

18. If you could change one thing about yourself, what would it be?

_____

_____

_____

_____

_____

19. What do you consider your greatest achievement?

_____

_____

_____

_____

20. If you were to die and come back as a person or a thing, what would it be?

_____

_____

_____

_____

21. Where would you most like to live?

_____

_____

_____

_____

_____

22. What is your most treasured possession?

_____

_____

_____

_____

_____

23. What do you regard as the lowest depth of misery?

_____

_____

_____

_____

_____

24. What is your favorite occupation?

_____

_____

_____

_____

_____

25. What is your most marked characteristic?

_____

_____

_____

_____

_____

26. What do you most value in your friends?

_____

_____

_____

_____

_____

27. Who are your favorite writers?

_____

_____

_____

_____

_____

28. Who is your hero of fiction?

_____

_____

_____

_____

_____

29. Which historical figure do you most identify with?

_____

_____

_____

_____

_____

30. Who are your heroes in real life?

_____

_____

_____

_____

_____

31. What are your favorite names?

_____

_____

_____

_____

_____

32. What is it that you most dislike?

_____

_____

_____

_____

_____

33. What is your greatest regret?

_____

_____

_____

_____

_____

34. How would you like to die?

_____

_____

_____

_____

_____

35. What is your motto?

_____

_____

_____

_____

_____

Proust Questionnaire by

1. What is your idea of perfect happiness?

_____

_____

_____

_____

_____

2. What is your greatest fear?

_____

_____

_____

_____

_____

3. What is the trait you most deplore in yourself?

_____

_____

_____

9. On what occasion do you lie?

_____

_____

_____

_____

_____

10. What do you most dislike about your appearance?

_____

_____

_____

_____

_____

11. Which living person do you most despise?

_____

_____

_____

_____

_____

12. What is the quality you most like in a man?

_____

_____

_____

_____

_____

13. What is the quality you most like in a woman?

_____

_____

_____

_____

_____

14. Which words or phrases do you most overuse?

_____

_____

_____

_____

_____

15. What or who is the greatest love of your life?

_____

_____

_____

_____

_____

16. When and where were you happiest?

_____

_____

_____

_____

_____

17. Which talent would you most like to have?

_____

_____

_____

_____

_____

18. If you could change one thing about yourself, what would it be?

_____

_____

_____

_____

_____

19. What do you consider your greatest achievement?

_____

_____

_____

_____

_____

20. If you were to die and come back as a person or a thing, what would it be?

_____

_____

_____

_____

_____

21. Where would you most like to live?

_____

_____

_____

_____

_____

22. What is your most treasured possession?

_____

_____

_____

_____

_____

23. What do you regard as the lowest depth of misery?

_____

_____

_____

_____

_____

24. What is your favorite occupation?

_____

_____

_____

_____

_____

25. What is your most marked characteristic?

_____

_____

_____

_____

_____

26. What do you most value in your friends?

_____

_____

_____

_____

_____

27. Who are your favorite writers?

_____

_____

_____

_____

_____

28. Who is your hero of fiction?

_____

_____

_____

_____

_____

29. Which historical figure do you most identify with?

_____

_____

_____

_____

_____

30. Who are your heroes in real life?

_____

_____

_____

_____

_____

31. What are your favorite names?

_____

_____

_____

_____

_____

32. What is it that you most dislike?

_____

_____

_____

_____

_____

33. What is your greatest regret?

_____

_____

_____

_____

_____

34. How would you like to die?

_____

_____

_____

_____

_____

35. What is your motto?

_____

_____

_____

_____

_____

Proust Questionnaire by

_____

1. What is your idea of perfect happiness?

_____

_____

_____

_____

_____

2. What is your greatest fear?

_____

_____

_____

_____

_____

3. What is the trait you most deplore in yourself?

_____

_____

_____

_____

_____

4. What is the trait you most deplore in others?

_____

_____

_____

_____

_____

5. Which living person do you most admire?

_____

_____

_____

_____

_____

6. What is your greatest extravagance?

_____

_____

_____

_____

_____

7. What is your current state of mind?

_____

_____

_____

_____

_____

8. What do you consider the most overrated virtue?

_____

_____

_____

_____

_____

9. On what occasion do you lie?

_____

_____

_____

_____

_____

10. What do you most dislike about your appearance?

_____

_____

_____

_____

_____

11. Which living person do you most despise?

_____

_____

_____

_____

_____

12. What is the quality you most like in a man?

_____

_____

_____

_____

_____

13. What is the quality you most like in a woman?

_____

_____

_____

_____

_____

14. Which words or phrases do you most overuse?

_____

_____

_____

_____

_____

15. What or who is the greatest love of your life?

_____

_____

_____

_____

_____

16. When and where were you happiest?

_____

_____

_____

_____

_____

17. Which talent would you most like to have?

_____

_____

_____

_____

_____

18. If you could change one thing about yourself,
    what would it be?

    _____

    _____

    _____

    _____

    _____

19. What do you consider your greatest
    achievement?

    _____

    _____

    _____

    _____

20. If you were to die and come back as a person
    or a thing, what would it be?

    _____

    _____

    _____

    _____

    _____

21. Where would you most like to live?

_____

_____

_____

_____

_____

22. What is your most treasured possession?

_____

_____

_____

_____

_____

23. What do you regard as the lowest depth of misery?

_____

_____

_____

_____

_____

24. What is your favorite occupation?

_____

_____

_____

_____

_____

25. What is your most marked characteristic?

_____

_____

_____

_____

_____

26. What do you most value in your friends?

_____

_____

_____

_____

_____

27. Who are your favorite writers?

_____

_____

_____

_____

_____

28. Who is your hero of fiction?

_____

_____

_____

_____

_____

29. Which historical figure do you most identify
with?

_____

_____

_____

_____

_____

30. Who are your heroes in real life?

_____

_____

_____

_____

_____

31. What are your favorite names?

_____

_____

_____

_____

_____

32. What is it that you most dislike?

_____

_____

_____

_____

_____

33. What is your greatest regret?

_____

_____

_____

_____

_____

34. How would you like to die?

_____

_____

_____

_____

_____

35. What is your motto?

_____

_____

_____

_____

_____

Proust Questionnaire by

_____

1. What is your idea of perfect happiness?

_____

_____

_____

_____

_____

2. What is your greatest fear?

_____

_____

_____

_____

_____

3. What is the trait you most deplore in yourself?

_____

_____

_____

_____

_____

4. What is the trait you most deplore in others?

_____

_____

_____

_____

_____

5. Which living person do you most admire?

_____

_____

_____

_____

_____

6. What is your greatest extravagance?

_____

_____

_____

_____

_____

7. What is your current state of mind?

_____

_____

_____

_____

8. What do you consider the most overrated virtue?

_____

_____

_____

_____

_____

9. On what occasion do you lie?

_____

_____

_____

_____

_____

10. What do you most dislike about your appearance?

_____

_____

_____

_____

_____

11. Which living person do you most despise?

_____

_____

_____

_____

_____

12. What is the quality you most like in a man?

_____

_____

_____

_____

_____

13. What is the quality you most like in a woman?

_____

_____

_____

_____

_____

14. Which words or phrases do you most overuse?

_____

_____

_____

_____

_____

15. What or who is the greatest love of your life?

_____

_____

_____

_____

_____

16. When and where were you happiest?

_____

_____

_____

_____

_____

17. Which talent would you most like to have?

_____

_____

_____

_____

_____

18. If you could change one thing about yourself, what would it be?

_____

_____

_____

_____

_____

19. What do you consider your greatest achievement?

_____

_____

_____

_____

_____

20. If you were to die and come back as a person or a thing, what would it be?

_____

_____

_____

_____

_____

21. Where would you most like to live?

_____

_____

_____

_____

_____

22. What is your most treasured possession?

_____

_____

_____

_____

_____

23. What do you regard as the lowest depth of misery?

_____

_____

_____

_____

_____

24. What is your favorite occupation?

_____

_____

_____

_____

_____

25. What is your most marked characteristic?

_____

_____

_____

_____

_____

26. What do you most value in your friends?

_____

_____

_____

_____

_____

27. Who are your favorite writers?

_____

_____

_____

_____

_____

28. Who is your hero of fiction?

_____

_____

_____

_____

_____

29. Which historical figure do you most identify with?

_____

_____

_____

_____

_____

30. Who are your heroes in real life?

_____

_____

_____

_____

_____

31. What are your favorite names?

_____

_____

_____

_____

_____

32. What is it that you most dislike?

_____

_____

_____

_____

_____

33. What is your greatest regret?

_____

_____

_____

_____

_____

34. How would you like to die?

_____

_____

_____

_____

_____

35. What is your motto?

_____

_____

_____

_____

_____

Proust Questionnaire by

_____

1. What is your idea of perfect happiness?

_____
_____
_____
_____
_____

2. What is your greatest fear?

_____
_____
_____
_____
_____

3. What is the trait you most deplore in yourself?

_____
_____
_____

_____

_____

4. What is the trait you most deplore in others?

_____

_____

_____

_____

_____

5. Which living person do you most admire?

_____

_____

_____

_____

_____

6. What is your greatest extravagance?

_____

_____

_____

_____

_____

7. What is your current state of mind?

_____

_____

_____

_____

8. What do you consider the most overrated virtue?

_____

_____

_____

_____

_____

9. On what occasion do you lie?

_____

_____

_____

_____

_____

10. What do you most dislike about your appearance?

_____

_____

_____

_____

_____

11. Which living person do you most despise?

_____

_____

_____

_____

12. What is the quality you most like in a man?

_____

_____

_____

_____

_____

13. What is the quality you most like in a woman?

_____

_____

_____

_____

_____

14. Which words or phrases do you most overuse?

_____

_____

_____

_____

_____

15. What or who is the greatest love of your life?

_____

_____

_____

_____

_____

16. When and where were you happiest?

_____

_____

_____

_____

_____

17. Which talent would you most like to have?

_____

_____

_____

_____

_____

18. If you could change one thing about yourself, what would it be?

_____

_____

_____

_____

_____

19. What do you consider your greatest achievement?

_____

_____

_____

_____

_____

20. If you were to die and come back as a person or a thing, what would it be?

_____

_____

_____

_____

_____

21. Where would you most like to live?

_____

_____

_____

_____

_____

22. What is your most treasured possession?

_____

_____

_____

_____

_____

23. What do you regard as the lowest depth of misery?

_____

_____

_____

_____

_____

24. What is your favorite occupation?

_____

_____

_____

_____

_____

25. What is your most marked characteristic?

_____

_____

_____

_____

_____

26. What do you most value in your friends?

_____

_____

_____

_____

_____

27. Who are your favorite writers?

_____

_____

_____

_____

_____

28. Who is your hero of fiction?

_____

_____

_____

_____

_____

29. Which historical figure do you most identify with?

_____

_____

_____

_____

_____

30. Who are your heroes in real life?

_____

_____

_____

_____

_____

31. What are your favorite names?

_____

_____

_____

_____

_____

32. What is it that you most dislike?

_____

_____

_____

_____

_____

33. What is your greatest regret?

_____

_____

_____

_____

_____

34. How would you like to die?

_____

_____

_____

_____

_____

35. What is your motto?

_____

_____

_____

_____

_____

Proust Questionnaire by

_____

1. What is your idea of perfect happiness?

_____

_____

_____

_____

_____

2. What is your greatest fear?

_____

_____

_____

_____

_____

3. What is the trait you most deplore in yourself?

_____

_____

_____

_____

_____

4. What is the trait you most deplore in others?

_____

_____

_____

_____

_____

5. Which living person do you most admire?

_____

_____

_____

_____

_____

6. What is your greatest extravagance?

_____

_____

_____

_____

_____

7. What is your current state of mind?

_____

_____

_____

_____

_____

8. What do you consider the most overrated
   virtue?

_____

_____

_____

_____

_____

9. On what occasion do you lie?

_____

_____

_____

_____

_____

10. What do you most dislike about your
    appearance?

_____

_____

_____

_____

_____

11. Which living person do you most despise?

_____

_____

_____

_____

_____

12. What is the quality you most like in a man?

_____

_____

_____

_____

_____

13. What is the quality you most like in a woman?

_____

_____

_____

_____

_____

14. Which words or phrases do you most overuse?

_____

_____

_____

_____

_____

15. What or who is the greatest love of your life?

_____

_____

_____

_____

_____

16. When and where were you happiest?

_____

_____

_____

_____

_____

17. Which talent would you most like to have?

_____

_____

_____

_____

_____

18. If you could change one thing about yourself, what would it be?

_____

_____

_____

_____

_____

19. What do you consider your greatest achievement?

_____

_____

_____

_____

_____

20. If you were to die and come back as a person or a thing, what would it be?

_____

_____

_____

_____

21. Where would you most like to live?

_____

_____

_____

_____

_____

22. What is your most treasured possession?

_____

_____

_____

_____

_____

23. What do you regard as the lowest depth of misery?

_____

_____

_____

_____

_____

24. What is your favorite occupation?

_____

_____

_____

_____

_____

25. What is your most marked characteristic?

_____

_____

_____

_____

_____

26. What do you most value in your friends?

_____

_____

_____

_____

_____

27. Who are your favorite writers?

_____

_____

_____

_____

_____

28. Who is your hero of fiction?

_____

_____

_____

_____

_____

29. Which historical figure do you most identify with?

_____

_____

_____

_____

_____

30. Who are your heroes in real life?

_____

_____

_____

_____

_____

31. What are your favorite names?

_____

_____

_____

_____

_____

32. What is it that you most dislike?

_____

_____

_____

_____

_____

33. What is your greatest regret?

_____

_____

_____

_____

_____

34. How would you like to die?

_____

_____

_____

_____

_____

35. What is your motto?

_____

_____

_____

_____

_____

Proust Questionnaire by
Daisy Fuentes

1. What is your idea of perfect happiness?

   Having my family together in health, wealth, and happiness.

2. What is your greatest fear?

   Seeing those I love suffer and not being able to help.

3. What is the trait you most deplore in yourself?

   My quick temper.

_____

_____

4. What is the trait you most deplore in others?

   <u>Lying, obsessive-compulsive behavior.</u>

   _____

   _____

   _____

   _____

5. Which living person do you most admire?

   <u>Dalai Lama.</u>

   _____

   _____

   _____

   _____

6. What is your greatest extravagance?

   <u>Taking trips with my family. And my car.</u>

   _____

_____

_____

_____

7. What is your current state of mind?

   Happy. _____

   _____

   _____

   _____

8. What do you consider the most overrated virtue?

   Modesty. _____

   _____

   _____

   _____

9. On what occasion do you lie?

Never . . . Now . . .

10. What do you most dislike about your appearance?

Aging and not being able to do anything about it.

11. Which living person do you most despise?

Nobody.

12. What is the quality you most like in a man?

Kindness.

13. What is the quality you most like in a woman?

Positivity.

14. Which words or phrases do you most overuse?

Fuck.

15. What or who is the greatest love of your life?

My dogs and my nephews.

16. When and where were you happiest?

Right now.

17. Which talent would you most like to have?

Perfect pitch.

18. If you could change one thing about yourself, what would it be?

   I can't think of anything.

19. What do you consider your greatest achievement?

   My career. Building my brand.

20. If you were to die and come back as a person or a thing, what would it be?

   Daisy Fuentes.

21. Where would you most like to live?

   Everywhere that has both mountains and
   ocean.

22. What is your most treasured possession?

   My dogs.

23. What do you regard as the lowest depth of misery?

   Losing someone I love.

24. What is your favorite occupation?

The scientists who find cures for horrible illnesses.

25. What is your most marked characteristic?

Loyalty.

26. What do you most value in your friends?

Loyalty and support.

27. Who are your favorite writers?

Marissa and myself.

28. Who is your hero of fiction?

Holly Golightly.

29. Which historical figure do you most identify with?

Cleopatra.

30. Who are your heroes in real life?

My parents.

31. What are your favorite names?

Charlie for a girl, Tyler for a boy.

32. What is it that you most dislike?

Pretense and bullying.

33. What is your greatest regret?

Being easily distracted in my youth.

34. How would you like to die?

I wouldn't like to die . . . I don't think.

35. What is your motto?

Sometimes less is just less.

Acknowledgments

$\mathcal{F}$ROM THE BOTTOM of my heart . . . gracias.

Judith Curr, Amy Tannenbaum, and everyone at Atria: Thank you for your support and trust in my vision. You're a sexy bunch!

Johanna Castillo: Your patience, guidance, and understanding have been invaluable. Thank you.

Ray McKigney: Thank you for being a great manager. We've been through so much. From good times with MTV to great times with my very own brand at Kohl's. . . . Thank you for all your hard work.

Kim Jakwerth: You got me invited to present on an award show in Monaco, you've put me on Oprah, I bathed you when you broke both wrists snowboarding . . . great memories. Thank you for your friendship and for the hardwork.

Steve Davioult: We became instant friends when we met on my first calendar shoot in '94, and you've been doing my hair and makeup ever since. You are a star, a true artist, truly the best at what you do. You light up every set you step foot on, and you've been making me laugh for over 15 years. Thank you for your friendship and for making me beautiful.

Marissa Matteo: You are a phenomenal writer, a brilliant author, a good friend, and a true Jersey girl. You are one of those unforgettable women I talk about in this book. Your collaboration on *Unforgettable You* has made writing my first book an unforgettable experience. You are truly talented, and funny as shit. I can't wait to celebrate with you when you win your first Oscar and your first Nobel Prize.

To all the unforgettable sexy superstars who contributed to my book . . . Cindy Crawford: You are an icon. You get more beautiful every time I see you. Flawless. Dr. Brian Weiss: You are brilliant. Your writings have inspired me to be a better person. Jenny McCarthy: You are beautiful, smart, inspiring, and funny as shit. Michael Rapaport: You are such a cool, talented guy. Martyn Lawrence Bullard: Darling, you are simply fabulous. Thank you all for your time; your generosity is so appreciated and will not be forgotten.

To my beautiful family and friends who contributed to my book: Rosana F. Brijbag: I still don't understand how such a pain in the ass little sister could grow up to be such a beautiful, loving, and talented creature. Thanks for keeping it real and for always making me laugh so hard that I can barely breathe. Also, thanks to you and Bernie for my stunning nephews. Maria Fuentes: My beautiful loving mami. I'm impressed and inspired by your strength and courage. I'm so proud of you. You are the best. Thank you for loving me. Amado Fuentes: My amazing dad. You are an extraordinary man and loving father. I'm very proud of you. You are the best. Thank you for loving me. Crissy Rodriguez: I know it doesn't sound possible, but you are more beautiful today than when you were eighteen. I'm so proud to have you as my friend. I hope we are still talking about the good old days, disco dancing, and making new memories when we're eighty. I love you all very much, thank you.

Barbara Tischner: You are a great business partner and an even better friend. I've learned so much from you. Thanks for your loyalty and for taking a chance on me.

Haim Dabah and the Daisy Fuentes team at Regatta: You are the force behind the name. You are amazing partners, and I could not do it without you. Thank you for all the hard work.

Jeffrey Barone: You've photographed me more than any other photographer. Thanks for the laughs and for always making me look good.

Paulie and everyone at MAPS: I always look forward to working with you. You are the best! Thanks you for your amazing energy.

Kevin Mansell, Don Brennan, Jack Boyle, Peggy Eskenasi, and everyone at Kohl's: You are phenomenal partners. Thank you for your support and for giving my brand such a great home.

Mary Li Vecchi: I was only sixteen and had NO life experience whatsoever. You were designing couture for Piero Dimitri and you were the coolest, most fashionable chick I'd ever seen. You opened up a whole new world for me by introducing me to the world of modeling and fashion. You had a profound effect on who I would become. Thank you for turning me into a "real" model. I don't know why you chose me, but I will be forever grateful that you did.

Piero Dimitri: My first ever modeling photo shoot, and my first ever runway show was for you. Thank you for giving me that opportunity, and for all the great advice.

Raquel Egas: You are such a beautiful, elegant, and generous lady. I don't know why you decided I should be on television but I'm so glad you saw what I couldn't. I got that first TV job as a weather anchor because of you and your husband, Ivan, and for that I will always be grateful.

Barbara Corcoran: I'll always remember you as a strong, chic, sophisticated powerhouse. I met you at such a vulnerable, young age. You taught me so much about television and about myself. Thank you for your guidance and for believing in me. You changed my life when you gave me my first job as a presenter on MTV Internacional, and I will never forget you.

Steve Leeds: You are such a great guy. You were there from the very beginning. Thank you for believing in me and for giving me the opportunity of a lifetime.

Tony Di Santo: Your sense of humor is so good it's almost wrong. We've come a long way from our early days traveling the world with MTV. You taught me so much about making TV and taking chances. Thank you for encouraging me to step outside my comfort zone and be a goofball. You always brought out the Jersey girl in me. I'm so proud of you, and I'm happy to still know you after all these years.